THIRD EDITION
ALL ABOUT THE USA
A Cultural Reader

Milada Broukal
Peter Murphy

PEARSON
Longman

All About the USA 3: A Cultural Reader, Third Edition

Pearson Education, 10 Bank Street, White Plains, NY 10606

Staff credits: The people who made up the *All About the USA 3* team, representing editorial, production, design, and manufacturing, are Wendy Campbell, Dave Dickey, Dana Klinek, Laura LeDréan, Melissa Leyva, Michael Mone, Rob Ruvo, Keyana Shaw, and Mark D. Van Ells.

Cover art: Pat Wosczyk

Photo credits: Page 1 Philadelphia Museum of Art/Corbis; **p. 6** David Rosenberg/Getty Images; **p. 11** Ariel Skelley/Blend Images/Corbis; **p. 16** Jed Share and Kaoru/Corbis; **p. 21** Bettmann/Corbis; **p. 26** moodboard/Corbis; **p. 31** Jon Zich/Getty Images; **p. 36** Strauss/Curtis/Corbis; **p. 41** Three Lions/Getty Images; **p. 46** Bob Krist/Corbis; **p. 51** Jeff Vanuga/Corbis; **p. 56** M Stock/Alamy; **p. 61** Bettmann/Corbis; **p. 66** JupiterImages/Comstock Premium/Alamy; **p. 71** Envision/Corbis; **p. 76** AP Photo/Charles Rex Arbogast; **p. 81** Richard Cummins/Corbis; **p. 86** Kevin Winter/Getty Images; **p. 87** Robyn Beck/Getty Images; **p. 91** Alan R Moller/Getty Images; **p. 96** North Wind Picture Archives; **p. 101** kolvenbach/Alamy; **p. 106** David Sutherland/Corbis; **p. 111** Jonathon Larsen/Shutterstock.com; **p. 116** AP Photo/Paul Sakuma; **p. 121** Carl & Ann Purcell/Corbis; **p. 126** Bruce Coleman Inc/Alamy; **p. 131** Adam Woolfitt/Corbis; **p. 136** Corbis; **p. 141** American Stock/Getty Images; **p. 146** Jan Bengtsson/Etsa/Corbis.

Text composition: Integra

Text font: 12/15 New Aster

Library of Congress Cataloging-in-Publication Data
Broukal, Milada.
    All about the USA / Milada Broukal.— 2nd ed.
        p.   cm.
Rev. ed. of: All about the USA, 1st ed. 1999.
Revised ed. will be published in 4 separate volume levels.
ISBN 0-13-613892-6 (student bk. with audio cd v. 1, : alk. paper)
ISBN 0-13-240628-4 (student bk. with audio cd v. 2, : alk. paper)
ISBN 0-13-234969-8 (student bk. with audio cd v. 3, : alk. paper)
ISBN 0-13-234968-X (student bk. with audio cd v. 4, : alk. paper)
  1. Readers—United States. 2. English language—Textbooks for foreign
speakers. 3. United States—Civilization—Problems, exercises, etc. I.
Murphy, Peter (Peter Lewis Keane), 1947- II. Milhomme, Janet. III.
Title.
  PE1127.H5B68 2008
  428.64—dc22
                                2007032614

ISBN-10: 0-13-234969-8
ISBN-13: 978-0-13-234969-7

1 2 3 4 5 6 7 8 9 10—CRK—12 11 10 09 08 07

CONTENTS

INTRODUCTION

All About the USA 3 is a low-intermediate reader for English language students. Thirty units introduce typical American people, places, and things, providing students with essential information about the USA and stimulating cross-cultural exchange. The vocabulary and structures used in the text have been carefully controlled to help students gain fluency and confidence.

Each unit contains:
- An opening photo and prereading questions
- A short reading passage
- Topic-related vocabulary work
- Comprehension of main ideas
- Comprehension of details
- Discussion questions
- A writing activity
- A *Did You Know…?* section offering a fun fact about the topic

The **PREREADING** questions are linked to the photo on the first page of each unit. They focus the students on the topic of the unit by introducing names, encouraging speculation about content, involving the students' own experiences when possible, and presenting vocabulary as the need arises.

The **READING** passage for each unit ranges from about 200 to about 350 words. Students should first skim the passage for a general idea of the content. The teacher may wish to deal with some of the vocabulary at this point. The students should then read the passage carefully as they listen to the audio CD. Listening while reading helps students to comprehend and retain information in the reading.

The two **VOCABULARY** exercises focus on the boldfaced words in the reading. *Meaning*, a definition exercise, encourages students to work out the meanings of the target words from the context. Within this group are collocations, or groups of words that are easier to learn together. The second exercise, *Use*, reinforces the vocabulary further by making students use the words in a meaningful, yet possibly different, context. This section can be done during or after the reading phase, or both.

There are two **COMPREHENSION** exercises. *Looking for Main Ideas* should be used in conjunction with the text to help students develop reading skills, and not as a test of memory. Students are asked to confirm the basic content of the text, which they can do individually, in pairs, in small groups, or as a whole class. *Looking for Details* expands the students' exploration of the text, concentrating on the scanning skills necessary to derive maximum value from reading.

The **DISCUSSION** section gives the students the opportunity to bring their knowledge and imagination to the topics and related areas. They can discuss the questions with a partner or in small groups. The teacher may ask students to report back to the class on a given question.

The **WRITING** section prompts students to write simple sentences or a short paragraph about a subject related to the topic of the unit. Teachers should use their own judgment when deciding whether to correct the writing exercises.

George Washington

PREREADING

Answer the questions.

1. Who is the president of the United States today?
2. Can you name any other American presidents?
3. Who is your favorite president or world leader? Why?

George Washington

In 1775, when the American War of Independence began, Congress chose George Washington to lead the American army. Washington knew his job would be difficult. The army was small. The soldiers were **untrained** and had few guns. The British army was large and strong. Its soldiers were very well trained.

The early **battles** showed Washington's problems. His army was easily **defeated** in the Battle of New York. Then Washington thought of a plan. On Christmas night in 1776, he had his soldiers attack the enemy in the city of Trenton, New Jersey. The enemy soldiers never expected an attack on such a night. They were having a Christmas party. Washington won his first **victory**. Washington's army won the final battle in Yorktown in 1781.

George Washington was a great leader and was **respected by** all his men. He was not interested in **fame** or money, but only in helping his country. There are many stories about George Washington. Many are probably not true. The most famous story, though, is about the cherry tree. It is said that young George cut down his father's cherry tree. When his father asked who cut down the tree, George **confessed** and said, "I cannot tell a lie."

In 1789, leaders from all the states met to choose the first president of the United States. The vote was **unanimous**. Everyone voted for George Washington. He became the country's first president and is remembered as the "Father of our Country."

VOCABULARY

⭐ **MEANING**

Complete the sentences with words from the box.

untrained	defeated	respected by	confessed
battles	victory	fame	unanimous

1. If you told someone you did something wrong, you _____.
2. If you are beaten, you are _____.

3. When people have a good opinion of someone else, he or she is

   _____ them.

4. When everyone agrees on a decision, the decision is _____.

5. If you have no practice doing a job, you are _____.

6. The events in which two armies fight are called _____.

7. People who are famous or well known have _____.

8. When an army wins, it is called a _____.

⭐ USE

Work with a partner to answer the questions. Use complete sentences.

1. What is the name of a person who has *fame*?
2. Who is a person who is *respected by* most people?
3. What job would be dangerous if you were *untrained*?
4. When is it a good idea to *confess* to something you did wrong?
5. What is something that all the students in your class will be *unanimous* about?
6. What team or famous sports player was *defeated* recently?

COMPREHENSION

⭐ LOOKING FOR MAIN IDEAS

Write complete answers to the questions.

1. What was George Washington's job during the War of Independence?

   _____

2. Why did people respect George Washington?

   _____

3. What happened to George Washington in 1789?

   _____

⭐ LOOKING FOR DETAILS

Circle *T* if the sentence is true. Circle *F* if the sentence is false.

1. Congress named George Washington president in 1775.   T   F
2. The British army was bigger than the American army.   T   F
3. The British soldiers were better trained than the
   American soldiers.   T   F
4. The Americans won all their battles.   T   F
5. The American soldiers had a party on Christmas
   in Trenton.   T   F
6. George Washington was not interested in fame or money.   T   F
7. The story about George Washington and the cherry
   tree is famous.   T   F
8. George Washington was the first president of
   the United States.   T   F

DISCUSSION

Discuss the answers to the questions with your classmates.

1. What do you know about our president?
2. What other world leaders can you name? What countries do they lead?
3. What qualities make a great leader?

4   UNIT 1

WRITING

Write six sentences or a short paragraph about a leader of a country.
If you write a paragraph, be sure to indent the first sentence.

EXAMPLE:

Nelson Mandela was the president of South Africa. He was the first black
president of that country.

_____

_____

_____

_____

_____

_____

DID YOU KNOW . . . ?

George Washington wore false teeth. They were made of ivory and not wood
as most people thought.

The Hot Dog

PREREADING

Answer the questions.

1. What is your favorite snack food?

2. What are some salty snack foods people eat in your country?

3. Why are snack foods so popular today?

The Hot Dog

In its home country of Germany, the hot dog was called the *frankfurter*. It was named after Frankfurt, a German city.

Frankfurters were first sold in the United States in the 1860s. Americans called frankfurters "dachshund sausages." A dachshund is a dog from Germany with a very long body and short legs. "Dachshund sausage" seemed like a good name for the frankfurter.

Dachshund sausages first became popular in New York, especially at baseball games. At games they were sold by men who kept them warm in **hot-water tanks**. As the men walked up and down the **rows of** people, they **yelled**, "Get your dachshund sausages! Get your hot dachshund sausages!" People got the sausages on a special kind of bread called a **bun**.

One day in 1906, a newspaper cartoonist named Tad Dorgan went to a baseball game. When he saw the men with the dachshund sausages, he **got an idea** for a **cartoon**. The next day at the newspaper office, he drew a bun with a dachshund inside—not a dachshund sausage, but a dachshund dog. Dorgan didn't know how to spell *dachshund*. Under the cartoon, he wrote "Get your hot dogs!"

The cartoon was a **sensation** and so was the new name. If you go to a baseball game today, you can still see sellers **walking around** with hot-water tanks. As they walk up and down the rows, they yell, "Get your hot dogs here! Get your hot dogs!"

VOCABULARY

⭐ **MEANING**

Complete the sentences with words from the box.

hot-water tanks	yelled	got an idea	sensation
rows of	bun	cartoon	walking around

1. The special kind of bread used for a hot dog is a _____.
2. Another word for *shouted* is _____.
3. When something is a cause of excitement, it is a _____.
4. Large containers of hot water, usually made of metal, are called _____.
5. A funny drawing is a _____.
6. Lines of people or objects are _____ people or things.
7. When you _____, you thought of or pictured something in your mind.
8. _____ is going here and there on foot.

⭐ **USE**

Work with a partner to answer the questions. Use complete sentences.

1. Where do you often see *rows of* people?
2. What movie is a *sensation* at this time?
3. What is your favorite *cartoon*?
4. What other things can you put in a *bun*?
5. Where can you find a *hot-water tank* other than at a baseball game?
6. Where can you see a lot of people *walking around*?

COMPREHENSION

⭐ LOOKING FOR MAIN IDEAS

Write the questions for the answers.

1. What _____?

   Americans called frankfurters "dachshund sausages."

2. Where in the United States _____?

   Dachshund sausages were first sold at baseball games.

3. Who _____?

   Tad Dorgan was a newspaper cartoonist.

⭐ LOOKING FOR DETAILS

Circle *T* if the sentence is true. Circle *F* if the sentence is false.

1. Frankfurters were first sold in the United States in
   the 1960s.   T   F
2. A dachshund is a dog with a long body and short legs.   T   F
3. At baseball games today you do not see sellers
   walking around with hot-water tanks.   T   F
4. Tad Dorgan got an idea for a cartoon in his office.   T   F
5. Tad Dorgan drew a bun with a sausage inside.   T   F
6. The words under Tad Dorgan's cartoon were
   "Get your hot dogs!"   T   F

DISCUSSION

Discuss the answers to the questions with your classmates.

1. Besides hot dogs, what are popular foods in the United States?
   What are some popular foods in your country?
2. Are hot dogs healthy for you? Why or why not?
3. What are some healthy foods? What are some foods that are not so
   healthy?

WRITING

Write six sentences or a short paragraph about a snack food or
sandwich you like. How do you make it? When do you eat it?
If you write a paragraph, be sure to indent the first sentence.

EXAMPLE:

My favorite snack food is a pita bread sandwich. I take a small

pita bread....

_____

_____

_____

_____

_____

_____

DID YOU KNOW . . . ?

New Yorkers eat more hot dogs than do people in any other city in the
United States.

Thanksgiving

PREREADING

Answer the questions.

1. Why do Americans celebrate Thanksgiving?
2. What kinds of food do people eat on Thanksgiving?
3. What are some symbols of this national holiday?

Thanksgiving

On the fourth Thursday in November, in houses around the United States, families get together for a feast, or a large meal. Almost all families eat turkey and cranberry sauce for this meal, and have pumpkin pie for **dessert**. This feast is part of a very special day, the holiday of Thanksgiving.

In 1620, the **Pilgrims** made a difficult trip across the ocean from England. They **landed** in what is now Massachusetts. In England the Pilgrims had not been allowed to practice their religion freely. So they went to the New World in search of religious freedom.

The Pilgrims' first winter was very hard. **Historians** say that almost half the group died of cold, hunger, and **disease**. But the Native Americans of Massachusetts taught the Pilgrims to plant corn, to **hunt**, and to fish. When the next fall came, the Pilgrims had **plenty of** food. They were thankful and had a feast to give thanks. They invited the Native Americans to join them. This was the first Thanksgiving.

Thanksgiving became a **national holiday** many years later because of a woman named Sarah Hale. For forty years Sarah Hale wrote to each president and asked for a holiday of Thanksgiving. At last she was successful. In 1863, President Lincoln declared Thanksgiving a holiday.

VOCABULARY

⭐ **MEANING**

Complete the sentences with words from the box.

dessert	landed	disease	plenty of
pilgrims	historians	hunt	national holiday

1. The last part of a meal is called the _____.

2. When a boat or an airplane has arrived from somewhere, we say it has _____.

3. People who travel from one place to another for religious reasons are _____.

4. If you feel sick, you may have a _____.

5. When you look for animals to kill for food, you _____.

6. If you have _____ something, you have more than you need.

7. When the government of a country celebrates a special day everywhere in the country, it is a _____.

8. _____ are people who write history.

⭐ USE

Work with a partner to answer the questions. Use complete sentences.

1. What is your favorite *dessert*?
2. What is the name of a *national holiday* in the United States or your country?
3. What city did you *land* in when you came to this country?
4. Why do people usually *hunt* animals?
5. What is the name of a *disease*?
6. What food is there *plenty of* at a Thanksgiving dinner?

COMPREHENSION

⭐ LOOKING FOR MAIN IDEAS

Write the questions for the answers.

1. When _____?

   Thanksgiving is celebrated on the fourth Thursday in November.

2. Who _____?

   The Pilgrims were religious people from England.

3. Why _____?

   They were thankful because they had food after a hard winter.

⭐ LOOKING FOR DETAILS

Number the sentences 1 through 8 to show the correct order.

_____ The Native Americans taught the Pilgrims to hunt and plant corn.

_____ In 1863, President Lincoln declared Thanksgiving a holiday.

_____ The Pilgrims left England in search of religious freedom.

_____ Sarah Hale asked every president to make Thanksgiving a national holiday.

_____ In 1620, the Pilgrims landed in Massachusetts.

_____ The Pilgrims invited the Native Americans to the first Thanksgiving.

_____ The Pilgrims' first winter was hard.

_____ Today, Thanksgiving is a day on which we give thanks.

DISCUSSION

Discuss the answers to the questions with your classmates.

1. What other American holidays do you know?
2. What holidays do you have in your country that are not celebrated in the United States?

14   UNIT 3

WRITING

Write six sentences or a short paragraph about how you celebrate a holiday in your country. If you write a paragraph, be sure to indent the first sentence.

EXAMPLE:

In Mexico, in November, we celebrate the Day of the Dead. We prepare

for this special day many weeks in advance.

_____

_____

_____

_____

_____

_____

DID YOU KNOW . . . ?

The first Thanksgiving celebration was in October and not November. It lasted for three days!

Blue Jeans

PREREADING

What do you know about the history of blue jeans?
Circle *T* (true) or *F* (false).

1. Levi Strauss was the first person to make blue jeans.   T   F
2. Levi Strauss was born in the United States.   T   F
3. Cowboys wore the first jeans.   T   F

Blue Jeans

Levi Strauss, a young **immigrant** from Germany, arrived in San Francisco in 1850. California was in the middle of the Gold Rush. Thousands of men were coming to California to dig for gold. Strauss came to sell canvas to these gold miners. Canvas is a **heavy fabric**. Strauss thought the miners could use the canvas for tents.

One day Strauss heard a miner **complain** that he couldn't find clothes strong enough for the work he was doing. Strauss got an idea. He quickly took some of his canvas and made it into pants. These pants were what the miners needed. In one day Strauss sold all the pants he had made.

Strauss wanted to improve his pants. He wanted to make them even better. He bought a fabric that was softer than canvas but just as strong. This fabric came from Nîmes, a city in France, and was called *serge de Nîmes*. The miners liked this fabric. They called it "denim" (from *de Nîmes*) and bought even more pants from Strauss.

However, denim had no color. Because of this the denim pants did not look very interesting, and they got dirty easily. To solve these problems, Strauss **dyed** the denim blue.

Strauss continued to improve his jeans. Today, the company he started is known around the world. People **consider** jeans to be not only **practical**, but very **fashionable as well**.

VOCABULARY

⭐ **MEANING**

Complete the sentences with words from the box.

immigrant	complain	consider	fashionable
heavy fabric	dyed	practical	as well

1. When people tell about their problems, they _____.
2. Clothes that are popular to wear are _____.
3. _____ is the same as *also* or *in addition to*.
4. A thick cloth-like canvas is a _____.
5. When you changed the color of something, you _____ it.
6. Many people think or _____ jeans to be fashionable.
7. A person who moves to another country is an _____.
8. When something is useful, it is _____.

⭐ **USE**

Work with a partner to answer the questions. Use complete sentences.

1. What is the name of an *immigrant* who came to this country and became famous?
2. What things are made from a *heavy fabric*?
3. Why do people *dye* things?
4. Where would you buy *fashionable* clothing today?
5. What is something that you use that is very *practical*?
6. What city or state in the United States do you *consider* to be a nice place to live?

COMPREHENSION

⭐ LOOKING FOR MAIN IDEAS

Write complete answers to the questions.

1. Why did Levi Strauss come to California?

   _____

2. What did the miners need?

   _____

3. How did Strauss improve his pants?

   _____

⭐ LOOKING FOR DETAILS

One **word in each sentence is** ***not*** **correct. Cross out the word and write the correct answer above it.**

1. Levi Strauss came to Germany in 1850.

2. There were thousands of men digging for canvas.

3. Levi Strauss came to buy canvas.

4. The miners needed clean pants.

5. Strauss made tents from denim.

6. Strauss got the denim from Germany.

7. Strauss dyed the denim red.

8. Levi's jeans are known all over the United States.

DISCUSSION

Discuss the answers to the questions with your classmates.

1. Do you think Levi Strauss was a good businessman? Why or why not?
2. If you could have your own business, what would it be?
3. What can clothes tell you about people?

WRITING

Write six sentences or a short paragraph about what you like to wear at home or at school. If you write a paragraph, be sure to indent the first sentence.

EXAMPLE:

At home I like to wear comfortable clothes. I usually wear jeans.

_____

_____

_____

_____

_____

_____

DID YOU KNOW . . . ?

Levi Strauss blue jeans with copper rivets* cost $13.50 per dozen in 1874.

**rivets:* short pieces of metal used to hold things together. On jeans, rivets strengthen the seams.

Alexander Graham Bell

PREREADING

Answer the questions.

1. What inventions do you use every day?

2. What do you think is the best invention? Why?

3. What kinds of telephones are there today? Which one is your favorite? Why?

Alexander Graham Bell

Alexander Graham Bell was born in 1847 in Edinburgh, Scotland. His father was an **expert** in phonetics, which is the study of the sounds of languages. As a boy, Bell became interested in sounds and speech.

In 1870, the Bells decided to come to America. They lived in Boston, where Alexander taught at a school for the **deaf**. There he began to **experiment** with a machine to help the deaf hear.

While experimenting with this machine, Bell had an idea. Why not use electricity to send the human voice from one place to another? Bell began work on a new invention.

For years, Bell and his assistant, Thomas Watson, worked day and night. They rented rooms in a **boardinghouse**. Bell was on one floor, and Watson was on another. They tried to send speech through a **wire**. Finally, on March 19, 1876, Watson heard these words very clearly: "Mr. Watson, come here. I want you." Watson **rushed** upstairs, ran into Bell's room, and shouted, "I heard you!"

That year was the centennial, or 100th birthday, of the United States. There was a large **fair** in Philadelphia called the Centennial Exposition. One of the **main attractions** at the exposition was Bell's "talking machine." Thousands of visitors, including Don Pedro, the emperor of Brazil, were surprised when they saw—and heard—this invention. But they still thought it was just an interesting toy. They didn't know that one day this talking machine would become the telephone and would change people's lives.

VOCABULARY

⭐ **MEANING**

Complete the sentences with words from the box.

expert	experiment	wire	fair
deaf	boardinghouse	rushed	main attractions

1. A person who is an _____ in a subject knows a lot about it and has training in it.
2. When you try new ideas, you _____.
3. The most interesting things to see somewhere are the _____.
4. When you went somewhere quickly, you _____.
5. A house with many rooms to rent is a _____.
6. A thin piece of metal is a _____.
7. People who are _____ cannot hear.
8. A show where people can see new things is a _____.

⭐ **USE**

Work with a partner to answer the questions. Use complete sentences.

1. What are the *main attractions* in your community?
2. What equipment has *wires*?
3. When do you usually *rush*?
4. Why do people stay in a *boardinghouse*?
5. What are some ways the *deaf* understand or "hear"?
6. What kinds of medicines do scientists *experiment* with?

COMPREHENSION

⭐ **LOOKING FOR MAIN IDEAS**

Circle the letter of the best answer.

1. As a boy, Bell was interested in sounds and speech because _____.
   a. he studied phonetics
   b. his father was an expert in phonetics
   c. he was born in Scotland

2. Bell and his assistant, Thomas Watson, _____.
   a. liked to live in a boardinghouse
   b. could not hear very clearly
   c. tried to send speech through a wire

3. _____ was one of the main attractions at the Centennial Exposition.
   a. Bell's "talking machine"
   b. Don Pedro, the emperor of Brazil,
   c. The large fair

⭐ **LOOKING FOR DETAILS**

Circle *T* if the sentence is true. Circle *F* if the sentence is false.

1. Alexander Graham Bell taught in a school for the deaf in Boston.	T	F
2. Bell and Watson worked together for years.	T	F
3. Bell and Watson were on the same floor in the boardinghouse in Boston.	T	F
4. Bell rushed upstairs and shouted, "I heard you!"	T	F
5. Don Pedro, the emperor of Brazil, was surprised when he saw the thousands of visitors.	T	F
6. Alexander Graham Bell came to America in 1870.	T	F

DISCUSSION

Discuss the answers to the questions with your classmates.

1. How did the invention of the telephone change people's lives?
2. How do you think the telephone will change in the future?
3. What ideas do you have for a new invention?

WRITING

Write six sentences or a short paragraph about an invention that has changed our lives. If you write a paragraph, be sure to indent the first sentence.

EXAMPLE:

Television has changed our lives in good ways and bad. Before television, we could not see far away events happen in front of our eyes.

_____

_____

_____

_____

_____

_____

DID YOU KNOW . . . ?
Alexander Graham Bell's mother and wife were both deaf.

UNIT 6
Body Language

PREREADING

Answer the questions.

1. How do you greet your friends?
2. How do you greet your teachers?
3. What are some gestures you often use?

Body Language

Sometimes people add to what they say even when they don't talk. Gestures are the "silent language" of every culture. We point a finger or move another part of the body to show what we want to say. It is important to know the body language of every country or we may be misunderstood.

In the United States, people greet each other with a handshake in a **formal** introduction. The handshake must be **firm**. If the handshake is weak, it is a sign of weakness or unfriendliness. Friends may place a hand on the other's arm or shoulder. Some people, usually women, greet a friend with a **hug**.

Space is important to Americans. When two people talk to each other, they stand about 2½ feet away at an **angle**, so they are not facing each other directly. Americans get uncomfortable when a person stands too close. They will move back to have more space. If Americans touch another person by accident, they say, "Pardon me," or "Excuse me."

Americans like to look the other person in the eyes when they are talking. If you don't do this, it means you are bored, hiding something, or not interested. But when you **stare** at someone, it is not polite.

For Americans, thumbs up means *yes*, *very good*, or *well done*. Thumbs down means the opposite. To call a waiter, raise one hand to head level or above. To show you want the check, make a movement with your hands as if you are signing a piece of paper. It is all right to point at things but not at people with the hand and **index finger**. Americans shake their index finger at children when they **scold** them and **pat** them on the head when they admire them.

Americans may use body language different from your own. Remember that each cultural group has its own gestures. The best thing to do is to learn not only the language but also the body language of other cultures.

VOCABULARY

MEANING

Complete the sentences with words from the box.

formal	hug	stare	scold
firm	angle	index finger	pat

1. A _____ greeting follows a certain custom or rule.

2. When you put your arms around people to greet them, you _____ them.

3. When you touch people or things lightly with the hand, you _____ them.

4. When you look at a person for a long time, you _____ at the person.

5. When you _____ people or animals, you tell them they are doing something wrong.

6. The finger next to your thumb is your _____.

7. When something is not straight, but set to one side, it is at an _____.

8. The opposite of soft and weak is _____.

USE

Work with a partner to answer the questions. Use complete sentences.

1. Whom do you *hug*?
2. Why do you *pat* someone?
3. When is an introduction *formal*?
4. Who *scolded* you when you were young?
5. What do you do when someone *stares* at you?
6. For which greeting(s) do you stand at an *angle*?

COMPREHENSION

⭐ **LOOKING FOR MAIN IDEAS**

Write complete answers to the questions.

1. What do people use to express themselves when they don't talk?

   _____ .

2. Why is it important to know the body language of a country?

   _____ .

3. Why do Americans stand at an angle when they talk to each other?

   _____ .

⭐ **LOOKING FOR DETAILS**

Circle the letter of the best answer.

1. In a formal introduction, Americans greet each other _____.
   a. with a hug
   b. with a handshake
   c. by placing a hand on each other's arm

2. When Americans talk to each other, they do not _____.
   a. face each other directly
   b. talk loudly
   c. look at each other directly

3. Americans feel uncomfortable when a person _____.
   a. stands too close
   b. points his or her thumb up
   c. looks them in the eyes

4. In the United States, if people touch each other by accident, they _____.
   a. move away
   b. stare at each other
   c. say, "Excuse me"

DISCUSSION

Discuss the answers to the questions with your classmates.

1. What American customs seem strange to you?
2. What are the rules about greeting people in your country? When do you shake hands? When do you kiss? How do you say good-bye?
3. What are two examples of body language that have different meanings in different countries?

WRITING

Write six sentences or a short paragraph about advice you would give someone coming to live and work in your country. If you write a paragraph, be sure to indent the first sentence.

EXAMPLE:

> *In Japan, we have strict rules about business behavior. You must exchange business cards immediately when you meet. You must read the card, but you should not put it in your pocket.*

_____

_____

_____

_____

_____

_____

DID YOU KNOW . . . ?

In Japan, women cover their mouths when they laugh because it is rude to show their teeth.

Mia Hamm

PREREADING

What do you know about soccer? Circle *T* (true) or *F* (false).

1. Only eleven players can play on each team at the same time.   T   F
2. Any player can pick the ball up and run with it.   T   F
3. A soccer game lasts for ninety minutes.   T   F

Mia Hamm

Mia Hamm is the best-known American soccer player in the world. She was a star player on the U.S. women's soccer teams that won two world **championships** and two Olympic gold **medals**. She also broke the record for scoring the most goals—for both women and men.

Mia Hamm was born in Alabama in 1972. Her father was an Air Force pilot so the family **moved** a lot. When Mia was very young, they lived in Italy for a while. Italians love soccer, and so did Mia. When they returned to the United States, Mia continued to play soccer. She even **joined** the boys' soccer team at school. The boys didn't mind because she was a good player.

At age fifteen, she was on the U.S. national women's team. She was the youngest player on the team. It was hard for her at first, but with hard work she soon became the best player. She told her parents she would win the world soccer championship one day, but at that time women's soccer world championships didn't exist; they were only for men. In 1991, her **dream** came true. The World Soccer Organization finally decided to start a World Cup for women. By 1996, women's soccer had also become an Olympic sport. During the 1999 World Cup, the American team played against the **favored** Chinese team and won. More than 90,000 people were in the **stadium** in Los Angeles, and 40 million watched the game on television. This made it the most watched women's sporting event in history.

Mia got married in 2003 and **retired** from international soccer in 2004.

VOCABULARY

⭐ **MEANING**

Complete the sentences with words from the box.

championship	moved	dream	stadium
medals	joined	favored	retired

1. When you decided to live in a new house, you _____ there.

2. When you hope for something very special, you _____ about it.

3. The team that wins the most games in a year wins the _____.

4. The building in which a sport is played is called a _____.

5. When you stopped playing a sport after a long time, you _____ from it.

6. When you got together with others to play a sport, you _____ a team.

7. If you are expected to win, you are said to be _____ to win.

8. When a team wins a championship, the players often get _____.

⭐ **USE**

Work with a partner to answer the questions. Use complete sentences.

1. What are some things you *join*?
2. Why might someone be *favored*?
3. What activity might you *retire* from?
4. What is something you *dream* of?
5. What can you do to win a *medal*?
6. If you are in a *stadium*, why might you be there?

COMPREHENSION

⭐ LOOKING FOR MAIN IDEAS

Write complete answers to the questions.

1. Why is Mia Hamm famous?

   _____

2. What was Mia's dream?

   _____

3. What did Mia win?

   _____

⭐ LOOKING FOR DETAILS

***One* word in each sentence is *not* correct. Cross out the word and write the correct answer above it.**

1. Mia Hamm is a famous tennis player.

2. Mia won two Olympic silver medals.

3. Mia broke the gold scoring record.

4. Mia lived in Italy because she was very young.

5. Women's soccer became an Olympic medal in 1996.

6. Four million people watched the United States beat China on TV.

7. The American soccer team beat the Chinese team in the Olympics in 1999.

8. Mia retired in 2003.

DISCUSSION

Discuss the answers to the questions with your classmates.

1. Why is soccer such a popular sport worldwide?
2. Why is soccer not as popular in the United States as other sports?
3. Will mixed teams of men and women ever play international soccer?

WRITING

Write six sentences or a short paragraph about your favorite sport. If you write a paragraph, be sure to indent the first sentence.

EXAMPLE:

My favorite sport is table tennis. I like it because . . .

_____

_____

_____

_____

_____

_____

DID YOU KNOW . . . ?

More than 6 million girls and women play soccer in the United States today, and the number continues to grow.

The American Cowboy

PREREADING

Answer the questions.

1. What did cowboys do?
2. Where did cowboys live?
3. Why is the cowboy an American hero?

The American Cowboy

The cowboy is the **hero** of many movies. He is a symbol of **courage** and **adventure**. But what was the life of an early American cowboy really like?

The cowboy's job is clear from the word *cowboy*. Cowboys were men who **took care of** cows and other cattle. The cattle were in the West and in Texas. People in the cities of the East wanted beef from these cattle. Trains could take the cattle east. But first the cattle had to get to the trains. Part of the cowboy's job was to take the cattle hundreds of miles to the railroad towns.

The trips were called cattle drives. A **cattle drive** usually took several months. Cowboys rode for sixteen hours a day. Because they rode so much, each cowboy **brought along** about eight horses. A cowboy changed horses several times each day.

The cowboys had to **make sure** that the cattle arrived safely. Before starting on a drive, the cowboys **branded** the cattle. They burned a mark on the cattle to show who they belonged to. But these marks didn't stop rustlers,* so the cowboys had to protect the cattle. The cowboys guarded the cattle day and night and scared the rustlers away. Rustlers made the dangerous trip even more dangerous.

Even though their work was very difficult and dangerous, cowboys did not earn much money. Yet cowboys liked their way of life. They lived in a wild and open country. They lived a life of adventure and freedom.

rustlers: people who steal cattle

VOCABULARY

⭐ **MEANING**

Complete the sentences with words from the box.

hero	adventure	cattle drive	make sure
courage	took care of	brought along	branded

1. If you looked after something and were responsible for it, you
   _____ it.
2. When you _____, you check to see everything is OK.
3. If you took things with you, you _____ these things.
4. When you are not afraid of something, you have _____.
5. When you do something new and exciting, you have an
   _____.
6. The main person in a movie or book is the _____.
7. When cowboys burned a mark into the cattle, they _____
   them.
8. When cowboys take a group of cows from one place to another, it is
   called a _____.

⭐ **USE**

Work with a partner to answer the questions. Use complete sentences.

1. When do you *take care of* friends or family?
2. Who is a popular movie *hero* today?
3. What do you *make sure* to do before you give work to your teacher?
4. When people invite you, is it a good idea to *bring along* a friend?
5. What kinds of people have the *courage* to do the things they do?
6. What was an *adventure* for you?

COMPREHENSION

⭐ LOOKING FOR MAIN IDEAS

Circle the letter of the best answer.

1. A cowboy is _____ .
   a. a symbol of courage and adventure
   b. not really a symbol
   c. a symbol of movies

2. The cowboy's job was to _____ .
   a. be a hero
   b. take care of cattle
   c. be a rustler

3. Cowboys _____ .
   a. made a lot of money
   b. had a difficult job
   c. did not like their way of life

⭐ LOOKING FOR DETAILS

***One* word in each sentence is *not* correct. Cross out the word and write the correct answer above it.**

1. Trains took the cattle west.

2. Cowboys rode for eight hours a day.

3. Each cowboy brought along about sixteen horses.

4. A cattle drive took several days.

5. The cowboys burned a mark on the rustlers.

6. The cowboys had to protect the rustlers.

7. People in the East wanted cowboys.

8. Cowboys were paid well.

DISCUSSION

Discuss the answers to the questions with your classmates.

1. What qualities do male heroes in movies and TV shows in your country have?

2. We often see cowboys and images of the old West in advertisements of American products such as trucks, blue jeans, and certain foods. Why do you think advertisers use cowboys to sell these products?

3. What is your impression of a cowboy's life? Would you like to live the life of a cowboy?

WRITING

Write six sentences or a short paragraph about a TV or movie hero. If you write a paragraph, be sure to indent the first sentence.

EXAMPLE:

I like Jackie Chan. He is my hero. In his movies, he . . .

_____

_____

_____

_____

_____

_____

DID YOU KNOW . . . ?
One in three cowboys was African American or Mexican.

Coca-Cola

PREREADING

**What do you know about the history of Coca-Cola?
Circle *T* (true) or *F* (false).**

1. In the beginning, Coca-Cola was a medicine.   T   F
2. People mixed Coca-Cola syrup with milk.   T   F
3. World War II made Coca-Cola popular worldwide.   T   F

41

Coca-Cola

In 1886, John Pemberton, a **druggist** in Atlanta, Georgia, made a brown syrup* by mixing coca leaves and cola nuts. Pemberton sold the syrup in his drugstore as a medicine to **cure** all kinds of problems. Pemberton called his **all-purpose** medicine "Coca-Cola."

When few people bought Coca-Cola, Pemberton sold the **recipe** to another druggist, Asa Candler. Candler decided to sell Coca-Cola as a soda-fountain drink instead of a medicine. At the soda fountains** in drugstores, the syrup was mixed with soda water to make the drink Coca-Cola. Candler advertised a lot and sold his syrup to many drugstores. Soon everyone was going to soda fountains and asking for Coca-Cola.

Candler saw no reason for putting Coca-Cola into bottles, but two businessmen thought this would be a good idea. They got permission from Candler, and **before long** they became millionaires.

As of 1903, coca leaves were no longer used in Coca-Cola. The exact **ingredients** used and their **quantities** are not known—the Coca-Cola Company keeps its recipe a **secret**.

World War I helped make Coca-Cola popular outside the United States. The Coca-Cola Company sent free bottles of the drink to U.S. soldiers fighting in Europe. Coca-Cola became very popular with the soldiers—so popular that the U.S. Army asked the company to start ten factories in Europe. After the war, these factories continued to make Coca-Cola. Today, there are Coca-Cola factories around the world.

*syrup: a sweet, heavy liquid that consists of flavor or medicine
**soda fountain: a place with a long counter where soda is served

VOCABULARY

⭐ **MEANING**

Complete the sentences with words from the box.

druggist	all-purpose	before long	quantities
cure	recipe	ingredients	secret

1. The different foods or things that are mixed together to make something are the _____.

2. When you do not tell something important to other people, you keep a _____.

3. A person who sells medicine is a _____.

4. A medicine can make you well and _____ your problem.

5. The _____ of things are the amounts.

6. What you follow to make a meal or drink is the _____.

7. Something that is good for many things is _____.

8. _____ is the same as *soon*.

⭐ **USE**

Work with a partner to answer the questions. Use complete sentences.

1. Which restaurant uses the best *ingredients* in its pizza?

2. What is a good and easy *recipe* you can share with the rest of the class?

3. What is your *cure* for a headache?

4. Where can you find an *all-purpose* medicine for pain?

5. What are you going to do *before long*?

6. What things do people keep a *secret*?

COMPREHENSION

⭐ LOOKING FOR MAIN IDEAS

Write complete answers to the questions.

1. How was Coca-Cola first used?

   _____

2. What did Asa Candler sell Coca-Cola as?

   _____

3. When did Coca-Cola begin to become popular around the world?

   _____

⭐ LOOKING FOR DETAILS

Number the sentences 1 through 8 to show the correct order.

_____ Today, there are Coca-Cola factories around the world.

_____ Few people bought John Pemberton's syrup.

_____ Asa Candler made Coca-Cola into a soda.

_____ Coca-Cola became popular in the United States.

_____ John Pemberton sold the recipe to Asa Candler.

_____ During World War I, the Coca-Cola Company sent Coca-Cola to U.S. soldiers in Europe.

_____ Two businessmen put Coca-Cola into bottles.

_____ A druggist, John Pemberton, invented Coca-Cola in 1886.

DISCUSSION

Discuss the answers to the questions with your classmates.

1. Why do people like soda?
2. Do you think soda is good for you? Why or why not?
3. Why do you think Coca-Cola is so popular around the world?

WRITING

Write six sentences or a short paragraph about how you prepare tea, coffee, or another drink. If you write a paragraph, be sure to indent the first sentence.

EXAMPLE:

In my country, Turkey, we make Turkish coffee. To make Turkish coffee you need very fine ground coffee, water, sugar, and a "cezve," a special pot in which to cook the coffee.

DID YOU KNOW . . . ?

In 1886, the first year Coca-Cola was sold, sales averaged nine drinks per day.

The Statue of Liberty

PREREADING

Answer the questions.

1. Where is the Statue of Liberty?
2. What doe the Statue of Liberty symbolize?
3. What is the name of another statue or monument in the United States?

The Statue of Liberty

One of the most famous statues in the world stands on an island in New York Harbor. This statue is, of course, the Statue of Liberty. The Statue of Liberty is a woman who holds a torch up high. It weighs 225 tons and is 301 feet tall.

The Statue of Liberty was put up in 1886. It was a gift to the United States from the people of France. **Over the years** France and the United States had a special **relationship**. In 1776, France helped the American colonies gain **independence** from England. The French wanted to do something special for the U.S. centennial, its 100th birthday.

Édouard-René Laboulaye was a well-known Frenchman who **admired** the United States. One night at a dinner in his house, Laboulaye talked about the idea of a gift. Among Laboulaye's guests was the French sculptor Frédéric-Auguste Bartholdi. Bartholdi thought of a statue of liberty. He offered to design the statue.

Many people **contributed** in some way. The French people gave money for the statue. Americans designed and built the pedestal* for the statue to stand on. The American people **raised money** to pay for the pedestal. The French engineer Alexandre Eiffel, who was famous for his Eiffel Tower in Paris, **figured out** how to make the heavy statue stand.

In the years after the statue was put up, many immigrants came to the United States through New York. As they entered New York Harbor, they saw the Statue of Liberty holding up her torch. She **symbolized** a welcome to a land of freedom.

*pedestal: the base on which a statue stands

VOCABULARY

⭐ **MEANING**

Complete the sentences with words from the box.

over the years	independence	contributed	figured out
relationship	admired	raised money	symbolized

1. When people or things have a connection with each other, they have a _____ .

2. _____ is another way of saying *during many years*.

3. If you understood something by thinking, you _____ something.

4. If something represented an idea, it _____ that idea.

5. If you respected and thought highly of someone, you _____ him.

6. If you joined with others to help to do something, you _____ .

7. When you collected money for something, you _____ .

8. To get free from someone or something is to gain _____ .

⭐ **USE**

Work with a partner to answer the questions. Use complete sentences.

1. Who is a person you *admire*?
2. Who do you have a good *relationship* with?
3. What have you learned *over the years*?
4. What country today has gained *independence* from another?
5. What are some things people *raise money* for?
6. When there is a disaster, such as an earthquake or tsunami, how do countries or people *contribute* to help?

COMPREHENSION

⭐ LOOKING FOR MAIN IDEAS

Circle the letter of the best answer.

1. The Statue of Liberty is a famous statue in _____.
   a. France
   b. the United States
2. The Statue of Liberty was a gift from _____.
   a. the people of France to the United States
   b. Laboulaye and Eiffel to the United States
3. The Statue of Liberty symbolizes a _____.
   a. woman with a torch
   b. land of freedom

⭐ LOOKING FOR DETAILS

Circle *T* if the sentence is true. Circle *F* if the sentence is false.

1. The Statue of Liberty is on an island.	T	F
2. The United States helped France gain its independence in 1776.	T	F
3. Alexandre Eiffel was a guest at Laboulaye's house.	T	F
4. Frédéric-Auguste Bartholdi was a French engineer.	T	F
5. Alexandre Eiffel figured out how to make the statue stand.	T	F
6. Americans designed the pedestal for the statue.	T	F

DISCUSSION

Discuss the answers to the questions with your classmates.

1. Do you have any famous statues or monuments in your country? What are they?
2. What famous statue, monument, or building do you think is the most beautiful or interesting? Which do you think is the ugliest?

WRITING

Write six sentences or a short paragraph about a famous statue, monument, or building. If you write a paragraph, be sure to indent the first sentence.

EXAMPLE:

The pyramids in Egypt are very interesting monuments. The pharaohs of Egypt had the pyramids built more than 5,000 years ago.

_____

_____

_____

_____

_____

DID YOU KNOW . . . ?

The Statue of Liberty had to be broken down into 350 pieces and packed in 214 boxes to get from France to New York.

The Bald Eagle

PREREADING

Answer the questions.

1. What are some animals around the world that are disappearing?
2. How can we stop animals from disappearing?
3. What are some animals that are symbols of countries?

The Bald Eagle

In 1782, soon after the United States won its independence, the bald eagle was chosen as the national bird of the new country. American leaders wanted the eagle to be a symbol of their country because it is a bird of strength and courage. They chose the bald eagle because it was found all over North America and only in North America.

But a little over 200 years later, the bald eagle had almost disappeared from the country. In 1972, there were only 3,000 bald eagles in the **entire** United States. The reason for the bird's **decreasing** population was **pollution**, especially pollution of the rivers by pesticides. Pesticides are chemicals used to kill insects and other animals that attack and destroy crops. Unfortunately, rain often washes pesticides into rivers. Pesticides pollute the rivers and poison the fish. Eagles eat these fish, and the poison **affects** their eggs. The eggs have very thin shells and do not **hatch**. Eagles **lay** only two or three eggs a year. Because many of the eggs did not hatch and produce more eagles, the number of eagles quickly became smaller.

Today, the American government and the American people are trying to **protect** the bald eagle. The number of bald eagles is increasing. It now appears that the American national bird will **survive** and remain a symbol of strength and courage.

VOCABULARY

⭐ **MEANING**

Complete the sentences with words from the box.

entire	pollution	hatch	protect
decreasing	affects	lay	survive

1. When eggs break and baby birds come out, the eggs _____.

2. When birds make eggs, they _____ them.

3. _____ means *complete* or *whole*.

4. To _____ something is to try to save it from harm.

5. When things continue to live under difficult conditions, they _____ .

6. There is _____ when the air or water is dirty.

7. When things are becoming smaller in number or size, they are _____ .

8. When something causes a change or a result, it _____ it.

⭐ USE

Work with a partner to answer the questions. Use complete sentences.

1. What other kinds of animals *lay* eggs?
2. How many students are there in the *entire* school?
3. What animals are *decreasing* in number?
4. In which cities do you find a lot of *pollution*?
5. How does pollution *affect* people?
6. How can a person *survive* in a desert?

COMPREHENSION

⭐ LOOKING FOR MAIN IDEAS

Write complete answers to the questions.

1. Why was the bald eagle chosen as the symbol of the United States?

   _____

2. Why did the bald eagle almost disappear from the country?

   _____

3. What are the American government and the American people trying to do for the bald eagle?

   _____

One word or number in each sentence is *not* correct. Cross it out and write the correct answer above it.

1. The United States won its independence after 1782.

2. British leaders wanted the eagle to be a symbol of their country.

3. They chose the bald eagle because it was found all over South America.

4. A little over 200 years late, the bald eagle had almost disappeared.

5. In 1972, there were only 30,000 bald eagles.

6. Unfortunately, rain often washes crops into rivers.

7. The eagles have very thin shells and do not hatch.

8. Today, the American government and the American people are trying to pollute the bald eagle.

DISCUSSION

Discuss the answers to the questions with your classmates.

1. Which animals are closely associated with your country?
2. If you could be an animal, what animal would you be? Why?
3. How are some animals useful to people?

WRITING

Write six sentences or a short paragraph telling a story about an animal. If you write a paragraph, be sure to indent the first sentence.

EXAMPLE:

One day a cat attacked one of our chickens. But the chicken did not die.

My mother took care of the chicken.

_____

_____

_____

_____

_____

_____

DID YOU KNOW . . . ?

Benjamin Franklin, a man responsible for the Declaration of Independence and the Constitution, was unhappy with the choice of the bald eagle as the symbol of the United States. He wanted it to be the wild turkey!

Baseball

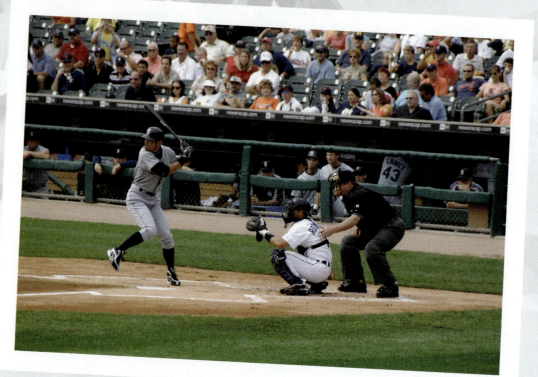

PREREADING

Answer the questions.

1. What sports do you think are "American"?

2. What do you need to play baseball?

3. What other things do you know about baseball?

Baseball

Baseball is the most popular sport in America. In a baseball game there are two **teams** of nine players. Players must hit a ball with a **bat** and then run around four **bases**. A player who goes around all the bases scores a run* for his team. The team that finishes with more runs wins the game.

Where did baseball come from? No one knows for sure. Many people believe that the idea came from a game played by children in England. Other people believe that a man named Abner Doubleday invented the game in Cooperstown, New York, in 1839. The first real **rules** of baseball were written in 1845 by Alexander Cartwright. Two teams from New York played a game following Cartwright's rules. The rules worked well. Soon there were many teams.

These early teams were not **professional**. They played only for fun, not money. But baseball was very popular from the start. Businessmen saw that they could make money with professional baseball teams.

The first professional team was started in 1869. This team was the Red Stockings of Cincinnati. Within a few years, there were professional teams in other cities. In 1876, these teams came together in a **league**, or group, called the National League. The teams in the National League played one another.

In 1901, a new league, called the American League, was formed. To create some excitement, in 1903, the two leagues decided to have their first-place teams play each other. This event was called the World Series.

Each year since then the National League winner and the American League winner play in the World Series. Each year, millions of people **look forward to** this exciting **sports event**.

a run: a score made in baseball when a player runs around all four bases

VOCABULARY

⭐ **MEANING**

Complete the sentences with words from the box.

teams	bases	professional	look forward to
bat	rules	league	sports event

1. When something important happens in sports, it is a

   _____ .

2. Teams that play a game the correct way are following the

   _____ .

3. A group of sports teams is called a _____ .

4. A wooden stick used to hit a ball is called a _____ .

5. The four stations the players must go around are _____ .

6. Groups of people who play together are _____ .

7. When teams play sports for money, they are _____ .

8. When you think happily about something that is going to happen,

   you _____ it.

⭐ **USE**

Work with a partner to answer the questions. Use complete sentences.

1. Which baseball *team* is the most popular in your community?
2. What is a *sports event* that you like to watch?
3. What are some *rules* of a sport that you know?
4. What do you use a *bat* for?
5. What is something you are *looking forward to*?
6. Who is your favorite *professional* sports player?

COMPREHENSION

⭐ LOOKING FOR MAIN IDEAS

Write the questions for the answers.

1. Where _____ ?

   No one knows where baseball came from, but the rules were written by Alexander Cartwright in 1845.

2. When _____ ?

   The first professional team was started in 1869.

3. Who _____ ?

   The National League winner and the American League winner play in the World Series.

⭐ LOOKING FOR DETAILS

Circle *T* if the sentence is true. Circle *F* if the sentence is false.

1. Baseball was invented in England.	T	F
2. Abner Doubleday played the game with Alexander Cartwright.	T	F
3. The early teams played for fun.	T	F
4. The Red Stockings were the first professional team.	T	F
5. In 1876 nonprofessional teams came together in a league.	T	F
6. The World Series has been played since 1903.	T	F
7. Baseball players must hit a ball with a bat and run around nine bases.	T	F
8. The winning teams in each league play each other in the World Series.	T	F

DISCUSSION

Discuss the answers to the questions with your classmates.

1. Do you like sports? Why or why not?
2. What is the most popular sport in your country?
3. If you could be a professional athlete, which sport would you play and why?

WRITING

Write six sentences or a short paragraph. Describe a sport you like to watch or play. If you write a paragraph, be sure to indent the first sentence.

EXAMPLE:

A sport I like is ice-skating. I cannot ice-skate, but I like to watch skating on television.

_____

_____

_____

_____

_____

_____

DID YOU KNOW...?

The longest baseball game in major league history was on May 1, 1920, between the Boston Braves and the Brooklyn Robins. The game lasted eight hours and twenty-two minutes and was finally called a tie with a score of 1–1.

John F. Kennedy

PREREADING

**What do you know about President John F. Kennedy?
Circle *T* (true) or *F* (false).**

1. John Kennedy came from a small family.   T   F
2. He was very athletic and strong as a child.   T   F
3. John Kennedy was popular because of his new ideas.   T   F

John F. Kennedy

In November 1960, John Fitzgerald Kennedy became the youngest man ever elected president of the United States. People liked him because he had new ideas. John Kennedy gave Americans hope for the future.

Kennedy was born on May 29, 1917. He was the second of nine children. His family was very **wealthy** and powerful. His father, Joseph, was so rich that he gave his children $1 million each when they reached the age of 21. Kennedy's mother, Rose, lived to the age of 104. Her religious **faith** and strength of character helped the family through its **tragedies** and **triumphs**.

As a child, Kennedy was sickly. He admired his brother Joe who was athletic and intelligent. Their father wanted Joe to be president one day, but Joe was killed during World War II. John was almost killed, too. A Japanese warship hit his boat, but he survived the crash. He won a medal for saving his men.

After the war, John Kennedy began a career in politics. When he became president, he gave a famous **speech**. He promised to work for freedom around the world. He asked people to give something of themselves. "Ask not what your country can do for you," he said. "Ask what you can do for your country."

Kennedy was very popular during his early presidency. People liked him and his wife, Jacqueline. She was young, beautiful, and **elegant**. People loved to see photos of the Kennedys with their two children, John and Caroline. They were the first children in the White House in fifty years.

Kennedy began the space program that put a man on the moon in 1969. He also started the Peace Corps. Thousands of young Americans volunteered to work where they were needed in countries around the world.

On November 22, 1963, John F. Kennedy was **assassinated** in Dallas, Texas. The world was filled with shock and **sorrow**.

VOCABULARY

⭐ MEANING

Complete the sentences with words from the box.

wealthy	tragedies	speech	assassinated
faith	triumphs	elegant	sorrow

1. Very sad events that shock people are called _____.

2. When people or things have beauty and style, they are _____.

3. When you have a lot of money, you are _____.

4. When you are sad, you feel _____.

5. Important victories are called _____.

6. When people are killed for political reasons, they are _____.

7. When you believe in something, you have _____ in it.

8. When you speak in front of a group of listeners, you give a _____.

⭐ USE

Work with a partner to answer the questions. Use complete sentences.

1. Who do you think is *elegant*?
2. How does a person become *wealthy*?
3. What do you have *faith* in?
4. Who is another politician who was *assassinated*?
5. What happened in the news that was a *tragedy*?
6. What has been a *triumph* in your life?

COMPREHENSION

⭐ LOOKING FOR MAIN IDEAS

Circle the letter of the best answer.

1. Americans voted for John F. Kennedy because _____.
   a. he came from a wealthy family
   b. he was still a young man
   c. they thought his ideas were good for the country

2. Kennedy wanted _____.
   a. more people to have careers in politics
   b. people all over the world to be free
   c. government to do more for the American people

3. During his presidency, Kennedy _____.
   a. began some important programs
   b. saved the lives of many people
   c. became wealthy and powerful

⭐ LOOKING FOR DETAILS

Number the sentences 1 through 7 to show the correct order.

_____ As a child, Kennedy was sickly.

_____ Kennedy was assassinated in Dallas, Texas.

_____ Kennedy became president.

_____ John F. Kennedy was born into a very wealthy and powerful family in America.

_____ Kennedy began the space program that put a man on the moon.

_____ Kennedy was almost killed when a Japanese warship hit his boat.

_____ Kennedy won a medal for his bravery.

DISCUSSION

Discuss the answers to the questions with your classmates.

1. Imagine you are president right now. What kinds of things would you do for the country?

2. John F. Kennedy wanted people to give something of themselves to their country. What kinds of things can people do to make their country a better place to live?

3. Who do you think makes a better leader, an older person with experience or a younger person with new ideas? Why?

WRITING

Write six sentences or a short paragraph. Give reasons why you would or wouldn't like to have a career in politics. If you write a paragraph, be sure to indent the first sentence.

> **EXAMPLE:**
>
> *I would not like to have a career in politics. First, it is too much responsibility.*

DID YOU KNOW...?

John F. Kennedy was the only president besides George Washington who did not want to take a salary as a president. He gave his salary to charity.

UNIT 14

The Gold Rush

PREREADING

Answer the questions.

1. What was the California Gold Rush?
2. Why is gold valuable?
3. What expressions in your language do you know that use the word *gold*? Translate them into English.

The Gold Rush

It was January 1848. A man was **digging** near the small village of San Francisco, California. Suddenly, he saw something **shiny**—gold!

By the next year, the California gold rush had begun. Thousands of men came to California. They were called "forty-niners," after the year 1849. The forty-niners came from all around the United States. They even came from other countries, including Mexico, Australia, China, France, and England. They left their families and jobs and made the difficult trip to California. They all **shared** a dream. They all wanted to make a **fortune** in gold.

Towns and camps grew quickly wherever gold was found. These towns were **rough places**. There was almost always a saloon, where the men drank and **gambled** for money with cards. In mining towns, men **stole** and sometimes killed for gold.

Did the miners make their fortunes? Some did, especially those who came early and were lucky. In 1848, miners usually made about $20 a day. In 1852, miners made about $6 a day. Many other people came to California to make money from the miners. Prices were very high. A loaf of bread, which cost 5¢ in New York, cost almost $1 in San Francisco.

In 1848, San Francisco was a village. Six years later, it was a city with a population of 50,000. In 1850, California had **enough** people to become a state.

VOCABULARY

⭐ MEANING

Complete the sentences with words from the box.

digging	shared	rough places	stole
shiny	fortune	gambled	enough

1. When something is bright with light, it is _____.
2. To make a lot of money is to make a _____.

3. Places that are dangerous and where people fight a lot are

_____.

4. When people played games such as cards for money, they

_____.

5. If you took things that belonged to other people, you _____.

6. If you had or used something with someone, you _____.

7. To have as much as is needed is to have _____.

8. When you are making a hole in the ground, you are _____.

USE

Work with a partner to answer the questions. Use complete sentences.

1. Who has made a *fortune*?
2. Why do some people *gamble*?
3. What is something *shiny*?
4. What is a *rough place* in your city?
5. When do people (or animals) *dig* in the ground?
6. What is something a person might *steal* from you?

COMPREHENSION

LOOKING FOR MAIN IDEAS

Circle the letter of the best answer.

1. In 1849, thousands of men came to California because they _____.
   a. were forty-niners
   b. wanted to find gold
   c. had families
2. Towns and camps grew _____.
   a. where there was gold
   b. where there was a saloon
   c. where there was no gold

3. Some of the miners who were lucky made _____.
   a. $20
   b. their fortune
   c. bread
4. In 1850, California _____.
   a. had a population of 50,000
   b. became a state
   c. had only one village

⭐ LOOKING FOR DETAILS

One **word or number in each sentence is** *not* **correct. Cross it out and write the correct answer above it.**

1. In 1848, a miner made $2 a day.

2. A loaf of bread cost 5¢ in England.

3. In 1854, San Francisco had a population of 500,000.

4. Some of the miners who came late were lucky.

5. Men gambled for cards in the saloons.

6. The forty-niners took their families and made the difficult trip to California.

DISCUSSION

Discuss the answers to the questions with your classmates.
1. How is gold used?
2. Are there any legends or stories about gold in your country's history? Tell the class.
3. Do people still value gold today? What other things do people consider of material value?

WRITING

Write six sentences or a short paragraph. What things have the greatest value for you? If you write a paragraph, be sure to indent the first sentence.

EXAMPLE:

It is nice to have a beautiful house and an expensive car. But the thing

that has the greatest value for me is my family.

DID YOU KNOW . . . ?

In California, there was not much water during the gold rush. Many forty-niners paid $100 for a glass of water!

UNIT 15

The Hamburger

PREREADING

Answer the questions.

1. What are some things you can get on a hamburger?
2. Why is the hamburger popular in the United States?
3. What other kinds of burgers can you eat?

The Hamburger

The hamburger has no connection to ham. It got its name from the German city of Hamburg, which was famous for its **ground** steak. German immigrants to the United States introduced the "hamburger steak."

At the St. Louis World's Fair in 1904, hamburger steaks were served on buns for the first time. Hamburgers on buns were **convenient** and tasted good. This became the usual way of eating hamburgers.

How did the hamburger become the most popular, most **typical** American food? The **introduction** of the bun is an important part of the answer. Another important part is McDonald's, the **fast-food** restaurant.

The first McDonald's was opened in San Bernardino, California, in 1949. Hamburgers were the **main item** on its menu. People liked the restaurant's fast service. By the 1960s, there were many McDonald's restaurants. McDonald's was a part of nearly every **community** in the United States. There were also other fast-food restaurants that sold hamburgers. McDonald's alone sold millions of hamburgers a year.

Today, of course, there are McDonald's restaurants around the world. The food they serve is considered typically American. Although McDonald's has **expanded** its menu, the main item on that menu is—as always—the hamburger.

VOCABULARY

⭐ MEANING

Complete the sentences with words from the box.

ground	typical	fast food	community
convenient	introduction	main item	expanded

1. _____ is food that is already prepared and sells quickly in a restaurant.

2. If something grew or became larger, it _____.

3. The most important thing of many on a list is the _____.

4. Something that is easy is _____.

5. Food, like steak or meat, that has been made into very small pieces is _____.

6. The people as a group in a town or area are a _____.

7. When something is common or represents something else, it is _____.

8. The _____ of something is when it is made known for the first time.

⭐ USE

Work with a partner to answer the questions. Use complete sentences.

1. What is your favorite *fast-food* restaurant?
2. What kinds of food can be *ground*?
3. Where can you find a restaurant in your *community*?
4. What food is *typical* of your country?
5. When is it a *convenient* time to eat?
6. What is the *main item* of the McDonald's menu?

COMPREHENSION

⭐ LOOKING FOR MAIN IDEAS

Circle the letter of the best answer.

1. The hamburger was _____.
   a. steak imported from Hamburg
   b. a ground steak introduced by immigrants
   c. a convenient bun

2. The American hamburger was different because it _____.
   a. had nothing to do with ham
   b. was convenient
   c. was served on a bun

3. McDonald's restaurants were partly responsible for _____.
   a. every community in the United States
   b. the introduction of the bun
   c. the hamburger's popularity

⭐ LOOKING FOR DETAILS

Write complete answers to the questions.

1. Who introduced the hamburger to the United States?

   _____

2. Where was the 1904 World's Fair?

   _____

3. How do most people eat hamburgers?

   _____

4. What do most people eat at McDonald's?

   _____

5. What do you call convenience foods like hamburgers?

   _____

6. Why is the hamburger considered a typical American food?

   _____

DISCUSSION

Discuss the answers to the questions with your classmates.
1. What types of fast food can you buy?
2. What are the advantages and disadvantages of fast food?
3. What do you think some fast foods of the future might be?

74 UNIT 15

WRITING

Write six sentences or a short paragraph about the most popular dish in your country. What is it made of? When do people eat it? If you write a paragraph, be sure to indent the first sentence.

EXAMPLE:

A popular dish in my country, Korea, is kim-chi. We eat kim-chi every day.

_____

_____

_____

_____

_____

_____

DID YOU KNOW . . . ?

McDonald's has spent millions of dollars on research on how to make perfect french fries. In 1957, McDonald's opened a research lab just for this!

Toni Morrison

PREREADING

Answer the questions.

1. What kind of writing do you like to read—novels, non-fiction, poetry, news?

2. Who is your favorite writer? Why?

3. What do you like to write about? Why?

Toni Morrison

Toni Morrison was born in 1931 in Ohio. She came from a hardworking family. She learned how to read early, and when she started school she was the only child in her class who could read. She was also the only black child in her class. Toni loved to read and was an excellent student. After she finished high school, she went to Howard University and received a bachelor's degree. Two years later, she received a Master of Arts degree from Cornell University and then returned to Howard to teach. While there she met Harold Morrison. They married and had two sons. **Unfortunately**, their marriage didn't work and they got divorced.

Toni moved with her sons to Syracuse, New York, and became a textbook **editor**. Later she became an editor for Random House, a **publishing** company in New York City. During her career as an editor she helped many black writers publish their books. She also started writing her own **novels**. She sent them to **various** publishers. They loved them and published them.

Both critics and the **public** have **praised** her novels. Most of her writing describes the experiences of African Americans. Her novel *Beloved* won the Pulitzer Prize for Fiction in 1988. It was **based on** a true story about a slave named Margaret Garner who killed her own daughter because she didn't want her to live as a slave.

In 1993, Toni Morrison received the Nobel Prize for Literature. She was the first African American woman and the eighth woman to win this important prize. Critics think she is one of the best writers of the twentieth century.

VOCABULARY

⭐ MEANING

Complete the sentences with words from the box.

unfortunately	publishing	various	praise
editor	novel	public	based on

1. A person who works with a writer to create a book is called an

   _____ .

2. People in general are often called the _____ .

3. Something sad or unlucky can be said to happen _____ .

4. To say nice things about people or their work is to _____

   them.

5. A long book that tells a story is a _____ .

6. When a book or movie develops from a true story, it is _____

   the story.

7. To try _____ things is to try a number of different ones.

8. The business of creating and selling books is called _____ .

⭐ USE

Work with a partner to answer the questions. Use complete sentences.

1. Have you read a book that is *based on* a true story?
2. What words of *praise* do you know to say to people?
3. What kinds of things in the news does the *public* like to know about?
4. What are *various* kinds of restaurants that people go to?
5. What is something *unfortunate* that happened to someone you know?
6. What is the name of a popular *novel*?

COMPREHENSION

⭐ ## LOOKING FOR MAIN IDEAS

Write the questions for the answers.

1. Who _____?

   Toni Morrison is a famous African American woman novelist.

2. Which book _____?

   Beloved won the Pulitzer Prize for Fiction in 1988.

3. When _____?

   She won the Nobel Prize for Literature in 1993.

⭐ ## LOOKING FOR DETAILS

Circle the letter of the best answer.

1. Toni Morrison was born in _____.
   a. Cornell
   b. Howard
   c. Ohio

2. Toni was the only _____ in her class.
   a. child
   b. black child
   c. family

3. Toni was the only child in her class who could _____.
   a. write
   b. love
   c. read

4. Toni received _____ university degrees.
   a. two
   b. three
   c. four

5. Toni worked as a _____ in Syracuse, New York.
   a. publisher
   b. teacher
   c. textbook editor

6. Critics think she is one of the _____ writers of the twentieth century.
   a. eighth
   b. best
   c. excellent

DISCUSSION

Discuss the answers to the questions with your classmates.

1. Who are some of the writers you know?
2. What would you like to write a book about?
3. Would you like to be a writer or an editor?

WRITING

Write six sentences or a short paragraph about a writer you know. Say what he or she writes about and why you like or dislike him or her. If you write a paragraph, be sure to indent the first sentence.

> **EXAMPLE:**
>
> *Toni Morrison is a great writer. I love how she takes events from real life and turns them into a novel.*

_____

_____

_____

_____

_____

_____

PREREADING

Answer the questions.

1. What is your favorite city? Why?
2. People associate gambling with Las Vegas. What do you associate with your favorite city?
3. What do tourists in your favorite city like to see?

Las Vegas

Las Vegas, Nevada, is the most famous city for gambling in the United States. Some people say that Las Vegas is a **mispronunciation** of "lost wages." The **casinos** and hotels have so many **neon** lights that some people call this city in the desert "The City of Lights."

Each of the big hotels in Las Vegas is special. Going into one is like entering another world. One hotel is like ancient Egypt. Another is like a tropical island. Still another is like New York City. These hotels have shows with famous entertainers. Everything looks expensive. But the rooms cost half the price of rooms in other places. And the restaurants have all-you-can-eat meals for very little money. That's because the hotels make their money from the casinos.

Las Vegas started in 1905 as a small train stop. There were only a few buildings in the middle of the desert. In 1946, a famous **gangster** named Bugsy Siegel built the first casino. He was murdered in 1947. This made him and Las Vegas more famous! In the early 1950s, tourists went to Las Vegas not only to gamble. They went to watch atomic bomb tests in the desert outside the city. In those days, people didn't know it was dangerous. They thought it was exciting.

Las Vegas is also famous for its many wedding **chapels**. Like all of Las Vegas, they are open twenty-four hours a day. Getting married is easy. A **couple** just pays a few dollars for a **license**, and they can get married immediately. They don't have to wait. Many famous movie stars were married in Las Vegas.

It is interesting that Las Vegas has more churches for its population than anywhere else in the United States. That's not counting wedding chapels. Another interesting fact is that tourists have a greater chance of having a **heart attack** in Las Vegas than in any other American city.

VOCABULARY

MEANING

Complete the sentences with words from the box.

mispronunciation	neon	chapels	license
casinos	gangster	couple	heart attack

1. A person who belongs to a group of criminals is a _____.

2. A condition in which a person's heart stops working is a

   _____ .

3. Two people who are married, engaged, or dating are a

   _____ .

4. _____ lights make Las Vegas very bright at night.

5. An official paper or card that gives permission to do something

   is a _____ .

6. _____ are buildings or rooms used for playing games to

   try to win money.

7. Making a mistake in how you say a word is a _____.

8. Rooms or small buildings used for a marriage, a funeral, or other

   religious services are _____ .

USE

Work with a partner to answer the questions. Use complete sentences.

1. A *chapel* is a religious building. What other religious buildings can you name?
2. What is a popular place a *couple* may go to after they get married?
3. What happens in a *casino*?
4. What things do you need a *license* for?
5. What does a *gangster* do?
6. What are *neon* signs used for?

COMPREHENSION

⭐ **LOOKING FOR MAIN IDEAS**

Write complete answers to the questions.

1. What is special about the hotels in Las Vegas?

   _____

2. Why is Las Vegas called "The City of Lights"?

   _____

3. What does Las Vegas have that other cities don't have?

   _____

⭐ **LOOKING FOR DETAILS**

Circle *T* if the sentence is true. Circle *F* if the sentence is false.

1. Some people think Las Vegas means "Lost Desert."	T	F
2. Las Vegas started as a farming town.	T	F
3. It costs a lot of money to stay in a hotel in Las Vegas.	T	F
4. A gangster named Bugsy Siegel built the first casino in Las Vegas.	T	F
5. No one wanted to go to Las Vegas after Bugsy Siegel was murdered.	T	F
6. It is easy to get married in Las Vegas.	T	F
7. In the 1950s, tourists went to the desert outside Las Vegas to see atomic bomb tests.	T	F

DISCUSSION

Discuss the answers to the questions with your classmates.

1. Certain cities do not allow gambling. Do you think this is a good idea? Why or why not?

2. Some people like to go to Las Vegas. Where do you like to go for fun? Why?

3. Why do you think tourists have a greater chance of having a heart attack in Las Vegas than in any other city in the United States?

WRITING

Do you think gambling is good or bad? Write six sentences or a short paragraph. Give your reasons. If you write a paragraph, be sure to indent the first sentence.

EXAMPLE:

I think gambling is bad. It is a waste of money.

_____

_____

_____

_____

_____

_____

DID YOU KNOW . . . ?
Las Vegas means "the Meadows" in Spanish.

The Oscars

PREREADING

Answer the questions.

1. Who are some celebrities who have won Oscars?

2. What kind of movies do you like — action, adventure, comedy, horror?

3. What other famous awards ceremonies can you name?

The Oscars

Since 1927, the Academy of Motion Picture Arts and Science has given annual awards to people for their **achievements** in the movie industry. At the awards **ceremony**, called the "Academy Awards" or "The Oscars," winners receive an Oscar—a small statue of a man holding a sword. The man is standing on a **reel** of film with five points on it. Each point represents a branch of the Academy: actors, writers, directors, producers, and technicians. Any of these people can receive an Oscar.

sword

reel

No one really knows how the name *Oscar* originated. The most popular story is that an **employee** named Margaret Herrick saw the statue and said, "Why, he looks just like my uncle Oscar." The name **stuck**, and it became official in 1939.

The Oscars ceremony has taken place in Hollywood since 1929 without exception. For many years, the ceremony took place in different hotels and theaters in Los Angeles. Finally, in 2001, the Kodak Theater was built in Hollywood as the **permanent** home for the ceremony. In 1929, the ceremony was only about fifteen minutes long, but today it takes several hours. In 2002, it lasted four hours and twenty-five minutes!

Thousands of people have received Oscars for their work in the movie industry. The person who has won the most Oscars is Walt Disney, with twenty-six. Three actors received Oscars for playing **roles** with no words at all. Some people have refused Oscars, some have been given Oscars after they have died, and one received an Oscar twenty years after his movie appeared.

The Oscars ceremony was shown for the first time on television in 1953. Every year, more than a **billion** people around the world watch it.

VOCABULARY

⭐ **MEANING**

Complete the sentences with words from the box.

achievements	reel	stuck	roles
ceremony	employee	permanent	billion

1. When a word like *Oscar* remained the same and did not change,

   it _____.

2. Important things that you succeed in doing on your own are

   _____.

3. Someone who works for and is paid by someone else is

   called an _____.

4. The wheel around which film is wound is called a _____.

5. If something is forever, it is said to be _____.

6. A formal celebration is called a _____.

7. A million million is called a _____.

8. The people actors play on screen are called _____.

⭐ **USE**

Work with a partner to answer the questions. Use complete sentences.

1. What is a *ceremony* you like to watch?
2. What are your favorite movie *roles*?
3. What is the difference between an *employee* and an employer?
4. How many zeroes are there in one *billion*?
5. What is something that is *permanent* in your life?
6. What has been your greatest *achievement*?

COMPREHENSION

⭐ **LOOKING FOR MAIN IDEAS**

Write the questions for the answers.

1. Why _____?

   People receive Oscars for their achievements in the movie industry.

2. What _____?

   It represents the five branches of the Academy of Motion Picture Arts and Science.

3. How long _____?

   The ceremony has taken place every year since 1929 without exception.

⭐ **LOOKING FOR DETAILS**

Circle *T* if the sentence is true. Circle *F* if the sentence is false.

1. An Oscar is an Academy.	T	F
2. Oscars are given for achievement in the movie industry.	T	F
3. An Oscar is a small man's uncle.	T	F
4. Oscars are given to five branches of the Academy.	T	F
5. The name Oscar became official in 1993.	T	F
6. Oscars are given at the Kodak Theater.	T	F
7. The ceremony has taken place since 1926.	T	F
8. Walt Disney has won the most Oscars.	T	F

DISCUSSION

Discuss the answers to the questions with your classmates.

1. Do you like the Oscars? Why or why not?
2. Who is your favorite actor? Why?
3. If you could be an actor, who would you be? Why?

WRITING

Write six sentences or a short paragraph. Describe your favorite movie. If you write a paragraph, be sure to indent the first sentence.

EXAMPLE:

My favorite movie is Home Alone. It is funny but serious, too.

_____

_____

_____

_____

_____

_____

DID YOU KNOW . . . ?

You can attend the Academy Awards only if you have an invitation. There are no tickets for sale to the public.

UNIT 19 Tornadoes

PREREADING

What do you know about tornadoes? Circle *T* (true) or *F* (false).

1. Tornadoes have winds that reach 300 miles per hour.   T   F
2. Tornadoes are common all over the world.   T   F
3. Tornadoes occur in the winter.   T   F

Tornadoes

Tornadoes are storms with very strong turning winds and dark clouds. These winds are perhaps the strongest on earth. They reach speeds of 300 miles per hour. The dark clouds are shaped like a **funnel**—wide at the top and narrow at the bottom. The winds are strongest in the center of the funnel.

Tornadoes are especially common in the United States, but only in certain parts. They **occur** mainly in the central states. A hot afternoon in the spring is the most **likely** time for a tornado. Clouds become dark. There is thunder, lightning, and rain. A cloud forms a funnel and begins to **twist**. The funnel moves faster and faster. The faster the winds, the louder the noise. Tornadoes always move in a northeasterly direction. They never last longer than eight hours.

A tornado's **path** is narrow, but within that narrow path, a tornado can destroy everything. It can smash buildings and **rip up** trees. Tornadoes can kill people as well.

The worst tornado **swept** through the states of Missouri, Illinois, and Indiana in 1925, killing 689 people. Modern weather equipment now makes it possible to **warn** people of tornadoes. People have a much better chance of protecting themselves. But nothing can stop tornadoes from destroying everything in their path.

VOCABULARY

⭐ MEANING

Complete the sentences with words from the box.

funnel	likely	path	swept
occur	twist	rip up	warn

1. Something that is probably going to happen is said to be
   _____.

2. To pull up violently is to _____.

3. Something that is wide at the top and narrow at the bottom is called a

   _____.

4. A storm that moved quickly and powerfully is said to have

   _____ through.

5. To move and turn around in a narrow space is to _____.

6. To tell of something bad before it happens is to _____.

7. A narrow way along which something moves is called a

   _____.

8. When something happens, it is said to _____.

USE

Work with a partner to answer the questions. Use complete sentences.

1. What might you *rip up*?
2. A *funnel* is a circular shape, wide at the top, narrow at the bottom. What are some other shapes you know?
3. What things are you *warned* of every day?
4. What other words for *path* do you know?
5. *Twist* describes a movement. What other movement words do you know?
6. When does the worst weather *occur* in your hometown?

COMPREHENSION

LOOKING FOR MAIN IDEAS

Write the questions for the answers.

1. What _____?

   They are storms with very strong winds and dark clouds.

2. Where _____?

   They are especially common in the central states.

3. When _____?

   The most likely time for a tornado to occur is a hot afternoon in the spring.

One word or number in each sentence is *not* correct. Cross it out and write the correct answer above it.

1. The winds are strongest in the center of the earth.

2. A tornado always moves in a southeasterly direction.

3. A tornado cannot kill people.

4. A tornado never lasts longer than eight days.

5. A tornado can reach speeds of 689 miles per hour.

6. Equipment can stop tornadoes from destroying everything in their path.

7. Clouds become hot in a tornado.

8. A tornado can kill buildings and rip up trees.

DISCUSSION

Discuss the answers to the questions with your classmates.

1. What other types of natural disasters can you name?
2. How can you prepare for natural disasters?
3. Why do you think people rebuild in places where natural disasters occur?

WRITING

Write six sentences or a short paragraph about a natural disaster you have seen or heard about. If you write a paragraph, be sure to indent the first sentence.

EXAMPLE:

A few years ago, there was an earthquake in Los Angeles. I was there at that time.

_____

_____

_____

_____

_____

_____

DID YOU KNOW . . . ?

A tornado destroyed a motel in Oklahoma and carried the motel's sign 30 miles away to Arkansas.

Lewis and Clark

PREREADING

What do you know about Lewis and Clark? Circle _T_ (true) or _F_ (false).

1. Lewis and Clark were explorers.   T   F
2. Native Americans helped Lewis and Clark.   T   F
3. Lewis and Clark sold tools.   T   F

Lewis and Clark

In 1803, the United States **doubled** in size when President Thomas Jefferson bought a huge piece of land from the French. It included all the land between the Mississippi River and the Rocky Mountains. This **deal** is known as the Louisiana **Purchase**.

Jefferson sent two army officers named Meriwether Lewis and William Clark to explore the new land. They led an **expedition** of about forty men. From St. Louis, they traveled up the Missouri River. Their purpose was to look for a **route** to the Pacific Ocean and find out more about this new land. Their voyage began in May of 1804.

On their travels across America, they had many adventures. In North Dakota, they made friends with Sacagawea, a **Native** American of the Shoshone tribe. She joined the expedition as a **guide**. She helped them get along with the native people they met during their trip. She knew where to find plants to eat and how to make tools. One time, as they crossed the Rocky Mountains, they almost **starved** and had to eat their horses. Luckily, a group of Native Americans helped them and gave them food.

In 1805, the expedition finally reached the Pacific Ocean and then turned around and came all the way back. In September 1806, Lewis and Clark returned to St. Louis. Many people thought they were dead because they had been gone for almost two and a half years. However, Lewis and Clark had discovered a way to the West and made friends with many of the Native American tribes. They immediately became national heroes.

VOCABULARY

 MEANING

Complete the sentences with words from the box.

doubled	purchase	route	guide
deal	expedition	native	starve

1. A business arrangement or agreement that is good for both sides is a _____.

2. A person born in a country is called a _____ of that land.

3. Something that grew two times bigger _____ in size.

4. Something you buy is called a _____.

5. A trip to explore a place is called an _____.

6. A way from one place to another is a _____.

7. If people die because they have no food, they _____.

8. Someone who shows you the road to follow is called a _____.

 USE

Work with a partner to answer the questions. Use complete sentences.

1. What is a recent *purchase* that you really like?
2. What is a good *deal* that you had?
3. What is the shortest *route* to your friend's home?
4. Why do people go on *expeditions*?
5. Where is your *native* land?
6. Where is a fun place to be a *guide*?

98 UNIT 20

COMPREHENSION

⭐ LOOKING FOR MAIN IDEAS

Write complete answers to the questions.

1. What was the Louisiana Purchase?

   _____

2. Whom did Jefferson send to explore the new land?

   _____

3. Which Native American guide helped the explorers?

   _____

⭐ LOOKING FOR DETAILS

One **word in each sentence is** *not* **correct. Cross out the word and write the correct word above it.**

1. The Louisiana Purchase halved the size of the United States.

2. The Louisiana Purchase excluded all land between the Mississippi River and the Rockies.

3. President Thomas Jenkinson made the deal.

4. Lewis and Clark were navy officers.

5. They led an exhibition up the Missouri River.

6. Their entire journey lasted three years and four months.

7. Sacagawea helped them fight with the Native Americans.

8. Lewis and Clark became national guides.

DISCUSSION

Discuss the answers to the questions with your classmates.

1. What other explorers do you know?
2. How do you think Lewis and Clark traveled all that way?
3. How far do you think they traveled?

WRITING

Write six sentences or a short paragraph. Describe your route to and from school. Include any transportation you use and the time it takes. If you write a paragraph, be sure to indent the first sentence.

EXAMPLE:

I start my trip to school from Jefferson Boulevard. I walk a couple of blocks east to Madison Street, and then I take the bus to Meriwether Park.

DID YOU KNOW . . . ?

When Lewis and Clark met Sacagawea she had a newborn baby. She took her baby on the trip all across America!

UNIT 21 Jazz

PREREADING

Answer the questions.

1. What different kinds of music can you name?
2. Where do you listen to music?
3. Where can you go to hear jazz?

Jazz

Americans have **contributed** to many art forms, but jazz, a type of music, is the only art form that was **created** in the United States. Jazz was created by black Americans. Many blacks were brought from Africa to America as **slaves**. The slaves sang and played the music of their **homeland**.

Jazz is a mixture of many different kinds of music. It is a combination of the music of West Africa, the work songs the slaves sang, and religious music. Improvisation is an important part of jazz. This means that the musicians make the music up as they go along, or create the music **on the spot**. This is why a jazz song might sound a little different each time it is played.

Jazz bands formed in the late 1800s. They played in bars and clubs in many towns and cities of the South, especially New Orleans. New Orleans is an international **seaport**, and people from all over the world come to New Orleans to hear jazz.

Jazz became more and more popular. By the 1920s, jazz was popular all over the United States. By the 1940s, you could hear jazz not only in clubs and bars, but in concert halls as well. Today, people from all over the world play jazz. Jazz musicians from the United States, Asia, Africa, South America, and Europe meet and share their music at **festivals** on every **continent**. In this way jazz continues to grow and change.

VOCABULARY

⭐ **MEANING**

Complete the sentences with words from the box.

contributed	slaves	on the spot	festivals
created	homeland	seaport	continent

1. People who are not free and are made to work for no pay are called _____.

2. One of the main masses of land on the earth is called a _____.

3. When something is first made, it is said to be _____.

4. A place where ocean ships come to is called a _____.

5. The country where you are born is your _____.

6. When you joined others and gave ideas to create something, you _____ to it.

7. Events where musicians meet to play and share their music are called _____.

8. To do something at the moment it happens is to do it _____.

⭐ USE

Work with a partner to answer the questions. Use complete sentences.

1. What is something you *created*?
2. What is the difference between a *slave* and an employee?
3. What is the name of a *seaport* town?
4. Where is your *homeland*?
5. What other types of *festivals* can you name?
6. How many of the *continents* of the world have you been to?

COMPREHENSION

⭐ LOOKING FOR MAIN IDEAS

Write complete answers to the questions.

1. What is jazz?

   _____

2. When did jazz become popular in the United States?

   _____

3. Who plays jazz today?

   _____

⭐ LOOKING FOR DETAILS

One word in each sentence is *not* correct. Cross out the word and write the correct answer above it.

1. Blacks were brought to Africa as slaves.

2. They sang the music of their bands.

3. Jazz festivals formed in the late 1800s.

4. Africa is an international seaport.

5. Improvisation is an important spot of jazz.

6. Jazz musicians share their music at festivals on every seaport.

DISCUSSION

Discuss the answers to the questions with your classmates.

1. What musical instruments are played in jazz bands?
2. What music is special to your country?
3. Who is your favorite musician or singer?

WRITING

Write six sentences or a short paragraph about the music you like.
If you write a paragraph, be sure to indent the first sentence.

EXAMPLE:

My favorite kind of music is classical music. My favorite composer is
Mozart.

DID YOU KNOW . . . ?

Boogie-Woogie, Bebop, and hard bop are all types of jazz.

Florida Oranges

PREREADING

Answer the questions.

1. What kinds of fruit can you grow in the United States?

2. Where do oranges grow?

3. What is your favorite kind of fruit? Why?

Florida Oranges

When the Spanish came to Florida around 1500, they brought orange trees with them. The oranges from these trees were not like the ones we enjoy today. They were small and **sour**. We must thank Lue Gim Gong, an immigrant from China, for the development of sweet oranges and other **citrus** fruit in Florida.

Lue Gim Gong lived on a farm in Canton, China, until he was twelve years old. Around 1870, he came to America with his uncle. He lived in San Francisco among many Chinese immigrants. Three years later he moved to Massachusetts and started working at a factory. He became friends with his English teacher, Miss Fannie Burlingame. He loved his life in America because of Miss Fannie. In 1877, he became an American citizen.

At twenty-six, Lue became ill with tuberculosis, a **lung** disease, and had to move to a warm **climate**. Miss Fannie told him to go to Florida where she and her sister owned orange **groves**. Lue started to work there and soon **developed** oranges that were very sweet and **juicy**. They were also strong, so they didn't die when there was a **frost**. About this time, Miss Fannie died and left the orange groves to Lue.

This new kind of orange was exactly what Florida orange growers needed. In 1911, Lue received the Wilder Silver Medal from the American Pomological Society for his work. This was the first time a medal was given for a citrus fruit.

Lue was a kind and generous man. He never became rich. Lue died in 1925. Today, the "Lue Gim Gong" orange is still grown in Florida.

VOCABULARY

⭐ MEANING

Complete the sentences with words from the box.

sour	lung	grove	juicy
citrus	climate	developed	frost

1. A _____ is a place where orange trees grow.

2. When the temperature goes below freezing, there is usually

   _____ .

3. Oranges with sweet liquid inside are said to be _____ .

4. Oranges belong to the _____ fruit family.

5. Before Lue Gim Gong, Florida oranges were not sweet but

   _____ .

6. Tuberculosis is a disease of the _____ .

7. _____ describes the type of weather you have.

8. Lue Gim Gong _____ a sweet orange.

⭐ USE

Work with a partner to answer the questions. Use complete sentences.

1. What is a fruit that is not *juicy*?
2. What fruits of the *citrus* family can you name?
3. What other *lung* diseases can you name?
4. What is the difference between sweet and *sour*?
5. Orange trees grow in *groves*. Where else do trees grow together?
6. What is the difference between *climate* and temperature?

COMPREHENSION

⭐ LOOKING FOR MAIN IDEAS

Write complete answers to the questions.

1. Who was Lue Gim Gong?

   _____

2. Where did Lue move to from Massachusetts?

   _____

3. What did Lue develop?

   _____

⭐ LOOKING FOR DETAILS

Write complete answers to the questions.

1. Who brought orange trees to Florida?

   _____

2. How did oranges taste in 1500?

   _____

3. How long did Lue stay in San Francisco?

   _____

4. When did Lue become an American citizen?

   _____

5. Who owned Lue's orange groves before him?

   _____

6. What medal did Lue receive for his work?

   _____

DISCUSSION

Discuss the answers to the questions with your classmates.

1. What food and drink do you know that tastes good with citrus fruit?
2. Why is citrus fruit good for your health?
3. What are some drinks and dishes you can make with oranges?

WRITING

Write six sentences or a short paragraph about the most popular fruit dish in your country. How is it made? When is it eaten? If you write a paragraph, be sure to indent the first sentence.

EXAMPLE:

A popular dish in my country, Mexico, is bananas with cinnamon and

Mexican chocolate. My mother makes this dish for me.

_____

_____

_____

_____

_____

_____

DID YOU KNOW ... ?

Florida produces about 75 percent of the United States's oranges and about 40 percent of the world's orange juice supply.

Mount Rushmore

PREREADING

Answer the questions.

1. Where is Mount Rushmore?
2. Why are the people on the monument famous?
3. What other large outdoor monuments do you know in other countries?

Mount Rushmore

Mount Rushmore is a 5,700-foot mountain in the state of South Dakota. The faces of four popular American presidents—George Washington, Thomas Jefferson, Abraham Lincoln, and Theodore Roosevelt—are **carved** into the mountain. These faces are known as the Mount Rushmore National **Memorial** and are the largest carved figures in the world.

An official from the Historical Society of South Dakota had the idea for a large monument. He wanted a monument of famous people from the Wild West to attract tourists to his state. He chose the **sculptor** Gutzon Borglum because he was famous for his huge statues. However, Borglum decided to carve the faces of four presidents, and everyone liked the new idea.

Borglum started the project in 1927. About 400 men worked on the mountain. The workers were strapped into special chairs. These chairs were lowered down the mountain with safety lines. Hanging from the side of the mountain, the workers drilled the stone. The work was slow and often difficult, especially in the winter months. However, no one on the project was killed or permanently **injured**. The work took fourteen years to complete. Borglum died **shortly before** it was done, and his son **took over** the project. The memorial was opened to the public in 1941. People were **amazed** to see the huge faces. Each one was as high as a six-story building!

The days of huge memorials like this are **not over**. Just 17 miles from Mount Rushmore, workers are drilling another mountain to carve a memorial for the Native American chief Crazy Horse. When it is complete, it will be the largest sculpture in the world.

VOCABULARY

⭐ **MEANING**

Complete the sentences with words from the box.

carved	sculptor	shortly before	amazed
memorial	injured	took over	not over

1. A person who carves wood or stone is a _____.

2. If you are very surprised, you are _____.

3. A _____ keeps the memory of a person or thing alive.

4. If you _____ something, you became responsible for something.

5. When wood or stone is cut by an artist, it is _____.

6. When something is not finished, it is _____.

7. When something happens just before another action, it happens _____ it.

8. When an animal or person is hurt, he or she is _____.

⭐ **USE**

Work with a partner to answer the questions. Use complete sentences.

1. When you listen to the news, what are you often *amazed* to hear?
2. What did you do *shortly before* you came to class?
3. What is the name of another famous *memorial*?
4. What is the name of another famous *sculptor*?
5. What is something that is *not over* yet?
6. What happened the last time you were *injured*?

COMPREHENSION

★ LOOKING FOR MAIN IDEAS

Write complete answers to the questions.

1. Which presidents do you see in the Mount Rushmore National Monument?

   _____

2. Who was the sculptor?

   _____

3. How long did it take to complete the memorial?

   _____

★ LOOKING FOR DETAILS

Circle the letter of the best answer.

1. Mount Rushmore is _____ .
   a. a memorial to a sculptor from South Dakota
   b. a mountain in South Dakota

2. Only the _____ of the presidents are carved into the mountain.
   a. faces
   b. bodies

3. Gutzon Borglum _____ .
   a. was a huge sculptor
   b. sculpted huge figures

4. The faces of the presidents were as high as a _____ building.
   a. sixty-story
   b. six-story

5. Work on the mountain was _____ .
   a. difficult in the winter
   b. slow in the summer

6. The workers' chairs were _____ the mountain.
   a. strapped to
   b. hung from the side of

7. Borglum's son _____ .

   a. died before the work was complete

   b. finished his father's work

8. The memorial for Crazy Horse will be _____ than the Mount Rushmore Memorial.

   a. bigger

   b. smaller

DISCUSSION

Discuss the answers to the questions with your classmates.

1. What unusual monuments can you name?
2. For which famous person would you design a monument? What would it be?
3. Is building monuments a good idea? Why or why not?

WRITING

Write six sentences or a short paragraph about a famous monument or memorial. If you write a paragraph, be sure to indent the first sentence.

> **EXAMPLE:**
>
> *The Vietnam Veteran's Memorial is a famous monument in Washington, D.C.*

_____

_____

_____

_____

_____

_____

DID YOU KNOW . . . ?
Almost half a million tons of granite were removed from the cliff to create the four faces on Mount Rushmore.

Bill Gates

PREREADING

Answer the questions.

1. Why is Bill Gates famous?

2. What does success mean to you?

3. Is money important to you? Why or why not?

Bill Gates

Personal computers, or PCs, are an important part of our everyday lives. Many people cannot imagine life without them. One of the most important people in making these machines work is Bill Gates.

Bill Gates was born in 1955 in Washington state. He grew up in a rich family. His parents sent him to private school. There he met his business partner, Paul Allen. When they were in the eighth grade, they were writing programs for business computers and making money.

In 1973, Gates was accepted to Harvard University. His parents were happy. They thought he would **get over** his **obsession** with computers and become a lawyer like his father. Two years later, Gates **dropped out** of Harvard to work on a computer program with his friend Allen. They worked eighteen hours a day in a **dormitory** room at Harvard. They were writing the program that would run one of the first personal computers. In 1975, they created a company called Microsoft to sell their product.

Allen became ill with cancer and left Microsoft in 1983. He recovered a few years later and started his own company. Meanwhile, Microsoft became a **giant** company. By 1990, at the age of thirty-four, Gates was the youngest billionaire in the history of the United States. He was the "King of **Software**." He **achieved** his success with a lot of hard work. For more than ten years, he worked sixteen-hour days seven days a week. He had a dream and the **will** to succeed. By 1997, he was the richest man in the world.

VOCABULARY

⭐ MEANING

Complete the sentences with words from the box.

get over	dropped out	giant	achieved
obsession	dormitory	software	will

1. If you got something by working hard, you _____ it.

2. A building where college students live is called a _____.

3. Something very big can be called _____.

4. If in time you stop worrying about something, you _____ it.

5. An uncontrollable interest in something is called an _____.

6. A strong wish to do something is called the _____ to do it.

7. Computer programs are also called _____.

8. If you stopped taking classes and didn't graduate, you _____.

⭐ USE

Work with a partner to answer the questions. Use complete sentences.

1. Why is it often a bad idea to *drop out of* school?

2. What is something you have an *obsession* with?

3. What *software* programs can you name?

4. What are some other *giant* companies?

5. How do you know if you have the *will* to succeed?

6. What is the best way to *get over* a problem?

COMPREHENSION

⭐ LOOKING FOR MAIN IDEAS

Write the questions for the answers.

1. Where _____?

   Bill Gates met his business partner in school.

2. Why _____?

   Bill Gates and Paul Allen created Microsoft because they wanted to sell their program for personal computers.

3. How _____?

   Bill Gates worked sixteen-hour days seven days a week for more than ten years.

⭐ LOOKING FOR DETAILS

Circle the letter of the best answer.

1. Bill Gates was born in _____.
   a. New York
   b. Washington state
   c. California

2. In 1973, Bill Gates was accepted to _____.
   a. Microsoft
   b. Harvard
   c. computer school

3. Bill Gates's parents wanted him to become a _____.
   a. computer programmer
   b. teacher
   c. lawyer

4. When Gates and Allen were in the eighth grade, they were writing programs for _____.
   a. business computers
   b. personal computers
   c. private schools

5. Paul Allen left Microsoft because _____.
   a. he wanted to start his own company
   b. he was ill
   c. he became rich
6. In 1990, Bill Gates became the youngest _____ in U.S. history.
   a. company president
   b. college student
   c. billionaire

DISCUSSION

Discuss the answers to the questions with your classmates.
1. What are some ways of getting rich?
2. If you were a billionaire, what would you do with your money?
3. The world has become very dependent on computers. Do you think this is a good thing? Why or why not?

WRITING

Write a short paragraph about a person who is or was successful. Tell the story of how the person became successful. Be sure to indent the first sentence.

EXAMPLE:

My uncle is a successful businessperson. He owns a factory in my country.

_____

_____

_____

_____

_____

DID YOU KNOW . . . ?
Bill Gates's house in the state of Washington is 66,000 square feet. It took seven years to build and cost $97 million.

UNIT 25

Henry Ford

PREREADING

Answer the questions.

1. Who was Henry Ford?
2. What are some well-known car companies?
3. What does the car of your dreams look like?

Henry Ford

Henry Ford was born in 1863 in Michigan. He grew up on a farm, but he did not want to become a **farmer**. He left school when he was sixteen. He wanted to make cars so he went to work as a **mechanic**.

In 1896, Ford built his first car. This car was very different from the cars of today. For example, its wheels were bicycle wheels.

In 1902, Ford built a car that won an important **race**. This car was the fastest car that had ever been built. It went 70 miles per hour. By then Ford had enough money to start the Ford Motor Company.

At this time, cars cost a lot of money. Only very rich people bought them. Ford had a dream. He wanted to **build** a car that many people could **afford**. Ford was sure that people would buy cars if they could afford them. He said, "Everybody wants to be **somewhere** he isn't."

Ford's plan was to make all his cars the same. Cars that are all the same take less time and less money to make. Then Ford could **charge** less money for these cars. In 1908, Ford produced his famous Model T Ford. The Model T sold for $850. This was much cheaper than other cars but still more than most people could pay.

One day Ford visited a meat-packing factory. There he saw animal **carcasses** being moved from one worker to another. Each worker had a particular job to do when a carcass reached him. Ford realized that he could use this assembly line method to build cars.

It took less than two hours to build a car on the assembly line. Before, it took fourteen hours. Ford was able to drop the price of the Model T to $265.

Ford's dream had come true. The Model T was now a car that many people could afford. By 1927, when Ford stopped making the Model T, more than 15 million of these cars had been sold.

VOCABULARY

⭐ **MEANING**

Complete the sentences with words from the box.

farmer	race	afford	charge
mechanic	build	somewhere	carcasses

1. The dead bodies of animals are called _____.
2. No place special is _____.
3. To make something from pieces is to _____ it.
4. If you have enough money to pay for something, you can _____ it.
5. Someone whose work is to grow food products and raise animals is called a _____.
6. A person who works with machines is called a _____.
7. To ask someone for money for something that is for sale is to _____ for it.
8. To try to go faster than someone else is to _____.

⭐ **USE**

Work with a partner to answer the questions. Use complete sentences.

1. A *mechanic* is a type of engineer. What other types of engineers can you name?
2. What are some things people *build*?
3. Where is *somewhere* you would like to be right now?
4. What are the fastest and slowest *races* you can think of?
5. How do you know if you can *afford* something?
6. What are places you know that don't *charge* for parking?

COMPREHENSION

⭐ LOOKING FOR MAIN IDEAS

Circle the letter of the best answer.

1. Henry Ford built _____.
   a. the first car
   b. the first bicycle
   c. a car with bicycle wheels
2. Henry Ford's dream was _____.
   a. to build an assembly line
   b. to build a car most people could afford
   c. to build a car that would win a race
3. Ford first saw an assembly line _____.
   a. at a meat-packing factory
   b. on a farm
   c. at the Ford Motor Company

⭐ LOOKING FOR DETAILS

Circle *T* if the sentence is true. Circle *F* if the sentence is false.

1. Henry Ford left school when he was sixteen.	T	F
2. Henry Ford made bicycle wheels on the farm.	T	F
3. Ford built a car that went 70 miles per hour.	T	F
4. Only very poor people bought cars.	T	F
5. Ford said, "Everybody wants to be what he isn't."	T	F
6. In 1908, the Model T cost more than most people could pay.	T	F
7. Before the assembly line, it took fourteen hours to build two cars.	T	F
8. Ford dropped the price of the Model T by $585.	T	F

DISCUSSION

Discuss the answers to the questions with your classmates.
1. Which car do you think is the most popular in the United States?
2. What do you think the car of the future will look like?
3. There are more and more cars on the roads every year. What can be done to solve traffic problems?

WRITING

Write six sentences or a short paragraph. What is the perfect car for you? What can it do? What does it look like? If you write a paragraph, be sure to indent the first sentence.

EXAMPLE:

The perfect car for me looks like a Ferrari. It is red.

_____

_____

_____

_____

_____

DID YOU KNOW . . . ?
At first workers didn't like the assembly line and started to quit their jobs. Ford doubled their wages to $5 a day. Then everybody wanted to work for him.

The Cranberry

PREREADING

What do you know about cranberries? Circle *T* (true) or *F* (false).

1. Cranberries are bitter.   T   F
2. Cranberries grow everywhere in the United States.   T   F
3. Cranberries get ripe in warm weather.   T   F

The Cranberry

The cranberry is a North American fruit that grows on a **bush**. The cranberry is small, round, red, and very **bitter**. Native Americans used the **berries** for food and medicine. When settlers first came from England in the 1600s, they liked these berries, too. The settlers had never seen the berries before. They decided to call them "crane berries" because birds called cranes ate them.

The cranberry bush does not grow everywhere in the United States. It grows only in special conditions in northern states like Massachusetts and Wisconsin. Cranberries **ripen** when the weather starts to become cold. We see cranberries in the stores in the fall. Many people eat cranberries as part of the feast of Thanksgiving in November.

Sometimes cranberries are cooked and made into a sauce or a jelly. Cranberries taste less bitter after they are cooked. Cranberry growers separate the best cranberries from all the rest. It's hard to recognize the best cranberries just by looking. So cranberry growers use a special method, which was developed by accident by a man named John Webb.

One day, as John Webb was taking a **container** of berries down some steps, he **spilled** the berries. While he was **picking** them up, he noticed something interesting. The bad berries had stayed on the top steps, and the best berries had bounced down all the way to the bottom. Today, cranberry growers use a seven-step test to separate berries. The best cranberries are the ones that **bounce** down seven steps!

VOCABULARY

Complete the sentences with words from the box.

bush	berries	container	picking
bitter	ripen	spilled	bounce

1. Small round fruits can be called _____.
2. A _____ is a small tree.
3. A carton or can that you put things in is called a _____.
4. When you are taking fruit off a bush, you are _____ it.
5. If something does not taste sweet or salty, it is said to be

   _____.

6. When fruit is getting ready to be eaten, it is said to _____.
7. To jump up and down like a ball is to _____.
8. When you dropped things out of a container, you _____

   them.

⭐ USE

Work with a partner to answer the questions. Use complete sentences.

1. Cranberries grow on a *bush*. What other fruit grows on a *bush*?
2. What is another fruit that is *bitter*?
3. What are some things that people often *spill*?
4. What is the difference between a *berry* and a *nut*?
5. What is a type of *container*?
6. How can you tell if a banana has *ripened*?

COMPREHENSION

⭐ LOOKING FOR MAIN IDEAS

Write complete answers to the questions.

1. What is a cranberry?

   _____

2. Where does the cranberry bush grow?

   _____

3. Who developed the special method of separating the best cranberries from all the others?

   _____

⭐ LOOKING FOR DETAILS

***One* word in each sentence is *not* correct. Cross out the word and write the correct answer above it.**

1. Cranberries taste more bitter after they are cooked.

2. John Webb noticed that the best berries had stayed on the top steps.

3. Cranberry growers use a seven-method test to separate berries.

4. The Americans decided to call the berries "crane berries."

5. Many people eat cranberries on Halloween.

6. Cranberries can be cooled and made into a sauce or jelly.

7. Cranberries are in the stores in the summer.

8. It's easy to recognize the best cranberries just by looking.

DISCUSSION

Discuss the answers to the questions with your classmates.

1. What are some of the typical fruits that grow in your country?
2. What foods do you associate with other feasts or holidays you know?
3. What other fruits are commonly part of a main meal?

WRITING

Write six sentences or a short paragraph. Describe a special fruit or vegetable in your country. Say how it is used. If you write a paragraph, be sure to indent the first sentence.

EXAMPLE:

The special fruit in my country, Armenia, is the pomegranate.

Pomegranates grow on trees. They are like big apples.

_____

_____

_____

_____

_____

_____

DID YOU KNOW . . . ?

Cranberries are an excellent source of Vitamin C and chemicals that may protect against cancer, heart disease, and other diseases.

UNIT 27

The White House

PREREADING

What do you know about the White House? Circle *T* (true) or *F* (false).

1. The president lives in the White House.   T   F
2. In the beginning, the White House was gray.   T   F
3. George Washington designed the White House.   T   F

The White House

In Washington, D.C., 1600 Pennsylvania Avenue is a very special address. It is the address of the White House, the home of the president of the United States.

Originally, the White House was **gray** and was called the Presidential Palace. It was built from 1792 to 1800. At this time, the city of Washington itself was being built. It was to be the nation's new capital city. George Washington, the first president, and Pierre-Charles L'Enfant, a French engineer, chose the place for the new city. L'Enfant then planned the city. The president's home was an important part of the plan.

A **contest** was held to **pick** a design for the president's home. An **architect** named James Hoban won. He designed a large three-story house of gray stone.

President Washington never lived in the Presidential Palace. The first people to live there were John Adams, the second president of the United States, and his wife, Abigail. Abigail Adams did not really like her new house. In her letters, she often complained about the cold. Fifty fireplaces were not enough to keep the house warm!

In 1812, the United States and Britain went to war. In 1814, the British invaded Washington. They burned many buildings, including the Presidential Palace.

After the war, Hoban, the original architect, **partially** rebuilt the president's home. To cover the marks of the fire, the building was painted white. Before long it became known as the White House.

The White House is one of the most popular **tourist attractions** in the United States. Every year more than 1.5 million visitors **go through** the rooms that are open to the public.

VOCABULARY

⭐ MEANING

Complete the sentences with words from the box.

originally	contest	architect	tourist attraction
gray	pick	partially	go through

1. Black mixed with white makes the color _____.
2. A place that people want to see or visit is a _____.
3. Something that is not done completely is _____ done.
4. A person who designs buildings is called an_____.
5. To go or pass from one room to another room is to _____ the rooms.
6. To choose something is to _____ it.
7. When something is first done, it is _____ done.
8. A small competition is a _____.

⭐ USE

Work with a partner to answer the questions. Use complete sentences.

1. What is a famous *tourist attraction* in or near your town?
2. What is your favorite *contest* on television?
3. What object around you is *gray*?
4. What rooms or spaces do you *go through* to get to your classroom?
5. What is the difference between an *architect* and a builder?
6. When you see the sun *partially* what does it look like?

COMPREHENSION

⭐ LOOKING FOR MAIN IDEAS

Write complete answers to the questions.

1. Who lives in the White House?

   _____

2. Why was the White House built in Washington?

   _____

3. Why did the original home of the president need to be rebuilt?

   _____

⭐ LOOKING FOR DETAILS

Circle the letter of the best answer.

1. The _____ is 1600 Pennsylvania Avenue.
   a. address of Washington, D.C.
   b. address of the White House
   c. original name of the White House

2. Originally, the Presidential Palace was _____.
   a. white
   b. black
   c. gray

3. The president's home and the city of Washington were built _____.
   a. by the British
   b. at the same time
   c. by the French

4. The first president to live in the Presidential Palace was _____.
   a. George Washington
   b. Abigail Adams
   c. John Adams

5. The Presidential Palace was burned down by _____.
   a. Abigail Adams
   b. James Hoban
   c. the British
6. The new presidential home was painted white to _____.
   a. attract tourists
   b. cover the marks of the fire
   c. please Abigail Adams

DISCUSSION

Discuss the answers to the questions with your classmates.
1. What other famous U.S. buildings can you name?
2. If you had to choose a new capital for the United States, what would you choose? Why?
3. Where does the leader of your country live?

WRITING

Write six sentences or a short paragraph about the building where the leader of your country lives or about your country's capital city. If you write a paragraph, be sure to indent the first sentence.

> **EXAMPLE:**
> *My country's capital city is Tokyo. It has a very big population.*

_____

_____

_____

_____

_____

DID YOU KNOW . . . ?
The White House has 132 rooms and 35 bathrooms.

UNIT 28 Uncle Sam

PREREADING

Answer the questions.

1. Who is the man in the poster?
2. What do you think of his clothes?
3. What is your idea for a symbol for the United States?

Uncle Sam

Uncle Sam is a tall, thin man. He's an older man with white hair and a white **beard**. He often wears a tall hat, a bow tie, and the stars and stripes of the American flag.

Who is this strange-looking man? Would you believe that Uncle Sam is the U.S. government? But why do we call the U.S. government Uncle Sam?

During the War of 1812, the U.S. government **hired** meat packers to **provide** meat to the army. One of these meat packers was a man named Samuel Wilson. He was a friendly and **fair** man. Everyone liked him and called him Uncle Sam.

Sam Wilson stamped the boxes of meat for the army with a large *U.S.*—for *United States*. Some government inspectors came to **look over** Wilson's company. They asked a worker what the *U.S.* on the boxes **stood for**. As a joke, the worker answered that these letters stood for the name of his boss, Uncle Sam.

The joke spread, and soldiers began saying that their food came from Uncle Sam. Before long, people called all things that came from the government "Uncle Sam's." "Uncle Sam" became a **nickname** for the U.S. government.

Soon there were drawings and cartoons of Uncle Sam in newspapers. In these early pictures, Uncle Sam was a young man. He wore stars and stripes, but his hair was dark and he had no beard. The beard was added when Abraham Lincoln was president. President Lincoln had a beard.

The most famous picture of Uncle Sam is on a **poster** from World War I. The government needed men to fight in the war. In the poster, a very serious Uncle Sam points his finger and says, "I want YOU for the U.S. Army."

VOCABULARY

⭐ MEANING

Complete the sentences with words from the box.

beard	provide	look over	nickname
hired	fair	stood for	poster

1. If letters or pictures represented something, they _____ it.
2. A _____ is a name that stands for a real name.
3. A _____ is a picture with printed information that is put on a wall.
4. A _____ person is a good person who does what he or she promises.
5. If you agreed to employ someone, you _____ that person.
6. Hair on a man's face is called his _____.
7. To examine or check something is to _____ it.
8. If you _____ something, you agree to make it possible for a person to have it.

⭐ USE

Work with a partner to answer the questions. Use complete sentences.

1. Uncle Sam is a *nickname*. What other *nicknames* do you know?
2. When the manager of a department store wants to *hire* a salesperson, what qualities does he or she look for?
3. Who is a famous person who has a *beard*?
4. What does your family *provide* you?
5. Why is it a good idea to *look over* your English homework?
6. A *poster* is a kind of advertisement. What other kinds of advertisements can you name?

138 UNIT 28

COMPREHENSION

⭐ **LOOKING FOR MAIN IDEAS**

Circle the letter of the best answer.

1. Everyone called Samuel Wilson _____.
   a. Uncle Sam
   b. a joke
   c. the United States

2. Uncle Sam is _____.
   a. the U.S. government
   b. the government meat packers
   c. the name of a government inspector

3. The most famous picture of Uncle Sam is _____.
   a. on a poster from World War I
   b. in a newspaper from World War I
   c. when he was in the army in World War I

4. In the early pictures of Uncle Sam, he _____.
   a. wears the stars and stripes
   b. has red hair
   c. has no hair

⭐ **LOOKING FOR DETAILS**

Circle *T* if the sentence is true. Circle *F* if the sentence is false.

1. Uncle Sam is short and thin.	T	F
2. Sam Wilson was a meat packer.	T	F
3. Everyone liked Sam Wilson.	T	F
4. Sam Wilson stamped the boxes "Uncle Sam."	T	F
5. The government inspectors asked Samuel Wilson what the *U.S.* on the boxes stood for.	T	F
6. "Uncle Sam" became a nickname for President Lincoln.	T	F

DISCUSSION

Discuss the answers to the questions with your classmates.

1. What are other symbols that represent the United States?

2. What other symbols for countries do you know?

3. How would you dress today's version of Uncle Sam?

WRITING

Write six sentences or a short paragraph about a famous world or country symbol. If you write a paragraph, be sure to indent the first sentence.

EXAMPLE:

The symbol of Thailand is the elephant. The shape of our country is like the shape of an elephant's head.

_____

_____

_____

_____

_____

_____

DID YOU KNOW . . . ?
Congress adopted Uncle Sam as a national symbol in 1961.

UNIT 29 Homesteaders

What do you know about homesteaders? Circle _T_ (true) or _F_ (false).

1. Homesteaders lived in the mountains.   T   F
2. A homestead was a kind of farm.   T   F
3. Homesteaders needed to be tough to be successful.   T   F

Homesteaders

Around 1860, towns started to grow in the West, but there was still a lot of unused land. So the Government **passed a law** called the Homestead Act in 1862. Under the new law, anyone over the age of twenty-one could **claim** 160 acres of land as long as he or she stayed on it for five years. The promise of free land brought thousands of people from the East to start their homesteads. They came to places like Kansas, Texas, Nebraska, Colorado, Wyoming, and the Dakotas. These states are in an area called the Great Plains because the land is flat and open.

Life was hard for the homesteaders. There was little water on the **plains** and it was difficult to raise **crops**. The farmers had oxen* to help them work the fields. Fires and bad weather such as **droughts** or **dust** storms often **destroyed** the crops. During difficult icy winters, when there was no food, the farmers had to kill and eat their oxen.*

There were not many trees on the plains, so there was no wood to build houses. Homesteaders made their houses by cutting squares of the earth. Then they used the sod** as **bricks** to make a house. The roof was made of dried grass or straw with more sod on it. The floor was just earth, and the windows were made of oiled paper.

Some homesteaders found farm life on the plains too difficult and moved farther west; others returned back to the East. Many homesteaders, however, stayed on their farms and did well.

*oxen: large cattle used for work on farms
**sod: the surface of the earth with grass and roots growing on it

VOCABULARY

⭐ MEANING

Complete the sentences with words from the box.

passed a law	plains	droughts	destroyed
claim	crops	dust	bricks

1. Billions of tiny pieces of earth that blow in the wind are called
   _____ .

2. Bad weather often killed the crops or _____ them. There
   were no more crops.

3. _____ are used to build houses or walls.

4. Long periods of dry weather are called _____ .

5. _____ are the fruits and vegetables farmers grow.

6. Big flat open areas of land with no trees are called _____ .

7. When you say you have the right to receive or own something,
   you _____ it.

8. When government leaders agreed to do something, they
   _____ on it.

⭐ USE

Work with a partner to answer the questions. Use complete sentences.

1. What other words for describing land, like *plains*, do you know?
2. Where can you see *bricks* in your town or neighborhood?
3. Farmers raise *crops*. What *crops* do you know of and what are they
   used for?
4. Natural disasters like *droughts* often destroy crops. What other natural
   disasters can you name and describe?
5. What kind of bad weather *destroyed* places or things recently?
6. Where do you find *dust*?

COMPREHENSION

⭐ **LOOKING FOR MAIN IDEAS**

Write the questions for the answers.

1. Who _____?

   Homesteaders were people who were promised free land.

2. Where _____?

   They came to the Great Plains.

3. What _____?

   They raised crops.

⭐ **LOOKING FOR DETAILS**

One **word in each sentence is** *not* **correct. Cross out the word and write the correct answer above it.**

1. There was a lot of used land in Kansas and Texas.

2. Under the Homestead Act of 1862, a person could claim 160 acres of land as long as he or she stayed on it for nine years.

3. People came from the Great Plains.

4. There was small water on the plains.

5. Crops were destroyed by bad floods.

6. Farmers had to freeze their oxen in hard times.

DISCUSSION

Discuss the answers to the questions with your classmates.

1. The Great Plains is the name of a group of U.S. states. What other names for groups of U.S. states do you know?
2. You are a new homesteader and just arrived on your land. What is your plan?
3. What was the problem with eating your oxen in a bad winter?

WRITING

Write six sentences or a short paragraph about one day as a homesteader. If you write a paragraph, be sure to indent the first sentence.

EXAMPLE:

This morning I got up at sunrise and had a breakfast of . . .

_____

_____

_____

_____

_____

_____

DID YOU KNOW . . . ?

In 1889, there was a land rush in the territory that is today the state of Oklahoma. A shot was fired and 100,000 settlers ran to claim land. It was all taken in a few hours!

UNIT 30 Kellogg's Corn Flakes

PREREADING

Answer the questions.

1. What is your favorite cereal? Why?
2. What do you like to eat for breakfast?
3. What are popular breakfast foods in your country?

Kellogg's Corn Flakes

What would breakfast be like without corn **flakes**? The inventor of corn flakes was Will Keith Kellogg. He was born in Michigan in 1860. He went to school, but left at the age of fourteen to work for his father. A few years later, he joined his brother John, who was a doctor at the Battle Creek Sanitarium. The sanitarium was a health center where ill people went to feel better. Will worked at the sanitarium doing **odd jobs** to help his brother.

Will also helped his brother to make new, healthy foods for his patients. One day, Will cooked some wheat to make special bread but forgot about it for several hours. When he came back the wheat wasn't good anymore, but he decided to put the wheat through rollers anyway. To his surprise, he noticed the grains became flakes. Will persuaded his brother to serve these flakes to his patients. The patients loved them. Will tried the same **process** with corn, and it worked even better.

By 1898, the brothers started a **mail-order** company selling corn flakes. However, John was not interested in the food business. Will continued on his own and started the Battle Creek Toasted Corn Flake Company. In a few years, Kellogg's Corn Flakes became a **household name**.

Will Kellogg became a millionaire, but he wasn't **comfortable** being rich. He continued to live in a two-story house, and didn't want his children to become rich by **inherited** money. He gave a lot of his wealth to many **charities**. In 1930, he started the W. K. Kellogg Foundation to help children, and in 1934, he gave more than $66 million to the Foundation. Will Kellogg died in 1951 at the age of 91. He worked at the Foundation until he died.

VOCABULARY

Complete the sentences with words from the box.

flakes	process	household name	inherited
odd jobs	mail order	comfortable	charities

1. A _____ is a thing or a person that everyone knows and speaks about.

2. Property or money left by someone who has died is _____.

3. _____ are organizations that help people in need.

4. Thin, dry, crisp pieces of food are called _____.

5. If you are _____, you are happy and satisfied.

6. When people sell products by mail, it is called _____.

7. Jobs that are not regular and change often are _____.

8. A way of doing something is a _____.

⭐ **USE**

Work with a partner to answer the questions. Use complete sentences.

1. What different types of breakfast *flakes* can you describe?
2. What is something you *inherited* from someone?
3. Which *charity* do you like most?
4. What person is a popular *household name*?
5. When don't you feel *comfortable*?
6. What steps do you have in your *process* for making coffee or tea?

COMPREHENSION

⭐ **LOOKING FOR MAIN IDEAS**

Circle the letter of the best answer.

1. Will Kellogg _____ corn flakes.
   a. invested
   b. invented

2. Will sold his corn flakes by _____.
   a. mail man
   b. mail order

3. Will gave a lot of his money to children _____.
   a. in need
   b. indeed

⭐ **LOOKING FOR DETAILS**

One **word in each sentence is** *not* **correct. Cross out the word and write the correct answer above it.**

1. At age fourteen, Will went to work for his brother.

2. His brother was a doctor at Roller Creek Sanitarium.

3. The Sanitarium was a rich center where people went to feel better.

4. Will worked doing strange jobs for his brother.

5. Will first invented corn flakes.

6. Will was surprised that the grains became dust.

7. Kellogg's Corn Flakes became a homestead name.

8. Will gave a lot of his money to family.

DISCUSSION

Discuss the answers to the questions with your classmates.

1. What is the difference between foods that are healthy and not healthy?
2. How do foods become popular?
3. What are the healthiest and the unhealthiest meals you can think of?

WRITING

Write six sentences or a short paragraph about your favorite breakfast. If you write a paragraph, be sure to indent the first sentence.

EXAMPLE:

My favorite breakfast is the one I have every day before school.

_____

_____

_____

_____

_____

_____

DID YOU KNOW . . . ?

Kellogg manufactures its products in 20 countries and distributes them in 160 countries.

ANSWER KEY

UNIT 1

VOCABULARY: MEANING

1. confessed   2. defeated   3. respected by
4. unanimous   5. untrained   6. battles
7. fame   8. victory

COMPREHENSION: LOOKING FOR MAIN IDEAS

1. George Washington's job was to lead the American army.
2. George Washington was a great leader who was not interested in fame or money.
3. George Washington became the country's first president.

LOOKING FOR DETAILS

1. F   2. T   3. T   4. F   5. F   6. T   7. T   8. T

UNIT 2

VOCABULARY: MEANING

1. bun   2. yelled   3. sensation
4. hot-water tanks   5. cartoon   6. rows of
7. got an idea   8. Walking around

COMPREHENSION: LOOKING FOR MAIN IDEAS

1. What did Americans call frankfurters?
2. Where in the United States were dachshund sausages first sold?
3. Who was Tad Dorgan?

LOOKING FOR DETAILS

1. F   2. T   3. F   4. F   5. F   6. T

UNIT 3

VOCABULARY: MEANING

1. dessert   2. landed   3. pilgrims   4. disease
5. hunt   6. plenty of   7. national holiday
8. Historians

COMPREHENSION: LOOKING FOR MAIN IDEAS

1. When is Thanksgiving celebrated?
2. Who were the Pilgrims?
3. Why were the Pilgrims thankful?

LOOKING FOR DETAILS

4, 7, 1, 6, 2, 5, 3, 8

UNIT 4

PREREADING

1. T   2. F   3. F

VOCABULARY: MEANING

1. complain   2. fashionable   3. As well
4. heavy fabric   5. dyed   6. consider
7. immigrant   8. practical

COMPREHENSION: LOOKING FOR MAIN IDEAS

1. Levi Strauss came to California to sell canvas to the gold miners.
2. The miners needed clothes strong enough for their work.
3. Strauss used a fabric that was softer than canvas but just as strong.

LOOKING FOR DETAILS

1. Germany → San Francisco
2. canvas → gold
3. buy → sell
4. clean → strong
5. tents → pants
6. Germany → Nîmes, a city in France
7. red → blue
8. United States → world

UNIT 5

VOCABULARY: MEANING

1. expert   2. experiment
3. main attractions   4. rushed
5. boardinghouse   6. wire   7. deaf   8. fair

COMPREHENSION: LOOKING FOR MAIN IDEAS

1. b   2. c   3. a

LOOKING FOR DETAILS

1. T   2. T   3. F   4. F   5. F   6. T

UNIT 6

VOCABULARY: MEANING

1. formal   2. hug   3. pat   4. stare
5. scold   6. index finger   7. angle   8. firm

COMPREHENSION: LOOKING FOR MAIN IDEAS

1. People use gestures, or body language.
2. It is important to know the body language so as not to be misunderstood.
3. Americans get uncomfortable when a person stands too close.

LOOKING FOR DETAILS

1. b 2. a 3. a 4. c

UNIT 7

PREREADING

1. T 2. F 3. T

VOCABULARY: MEANING

1. moved 2. dream 3. championship
4. stadium 5. retired 6. joined 7. favored
8. medals

COMPREHENSION: LOOKING FOR MAIN IDEAS

1. Mia is the best-known American soccer player in the world.
2. Mia's dream was the women's world soccer championships.
3. Mia won two world championships and two Olympic gold medals.

LOOKING FOR DETAILS

1. tennis → soccer
2. silver → gold
3. gold → goal
4. because → when
5. medal → sport
6. Four → Forty
7. Olympics → World Cup
8. 2003 → 2004 *or* retired → got married

UNIT 8

VOCABULARY: MEANING

1. took care of 2. make sure
3. brought along 4. courage 5. adventure
6. hero 7. branded 8. cattle drive

COMPREHENSION: LOOKING FOR MAIN IDEAS

1. a 2. b 3. b

LOOKING FOR DETAILS

1. west → east
2. eight → sixteen

3. sixteen → eight
4. days → months
5. rustlers → cattle
6. rustlers → cattle
7. cowboys → cattle
8. were → weren't *or* well → poorly

UNIT 9

PREREADING

1. T 2. F 3. F

VOCABULARY: MEANING

1. ingredients 2. secret 3. druggist
4. cure 5. quantities 6. recipe
7. all-purpose 8. Before long

COMPREHENSION: LOOKING FOR MAIN IDEAS

1. Coca-Cola was first used as a medicine.
2. Asa Candler sold Coco-Cola as a soda-fountain drink.
3. Coca-Cola became popular around the world during World War I.

LOOKING FOR DETAILS

8, 2, 4, 5, 3, 7, 6, 1

UNIT 10

VOCABULARY: MEANING

1. relationship 2. Over the years
3. figured out 4. symbolized
5. admired 6. contributed
7. raised money 8. independence

COMPREHENSION: LOOKING FOR MAIN IDEAS

1. b 2. a 3. b

LOOKING FOR DETAILS

1. T 2. F 3. F 4. F 5. T 6. F

UNIT 11

VOCABULARY: MEANING

1. hatch 2. lay 3. Entire 4. protect
5. survive 6. pollution 7. decreasing
8. affects

COMPREHENSION: LOOKING FOR MAIN IDEAS

1. The bald eagle is a bird of strength and courage.
2. The bald eagle almost disappeared because pollution poisoned the fish that eagles ate. The poison affected the eagles' eggs, and as a result, many did not hatch.
3. They are trying to protect the bald eagle.

LOOKING FOR DETAILS

1. after → before
2. British → American
3. South → North
4. late → later
5. 30,000 → 3,000
6. crops → pesticides
7. eagles → eggs
8. pollute → protect

UNIT 12

VOCABULARY: MEANING

1. sports event   2. rules   3. league   4. bat
5. bases   6. teams   7. professional
8. look forward to

COMPREHENSION: LOOKING FOR MAIN IDEAS

1. Where did baseball come from?
2. When was the first professional team started?
3. Who plays in the World Series?

LOOKING FOR DETAILS

1. F   2. F   3. T   4. T   5. F   6. T   7. F   8. T

UNIT 13

PREREADING

1. F   2. F   3. T

VOCABULARY: MEANING

1. tragedies   2. elegant   3. wealthy
4. sorrow   5. triumphs   6. assassinated
7. faith   8. speech

COMPREHENSION: LOOKING FOR MAIN IDEAS

1. c   2. b   3. a

LOOKING FOR DETAILS

2, 7, 5, 1, 6, 3, 4

UNIT 14

VOCABULARY: MEANING

1. shiny   2. fortune   3. rough places
4. gambled   5. stole   6. shared   7. enough
8. digging

COMPREHENSION: LOOKING FOR MAIN IDEAS

1. b   2. a   3. b   4. b

LOOKING FOR DETAILS

1. $2 → $20
2. England → New York
3. 500,000 → 50,000
4. late → early
5. cards → money *or* for → with
6. took → left

UNIT 15

VOCABULARY: MEANING

1. Fast food   2. expanded   3. main item
4. convenient   5. ground   6. community
7. typical   8. introduction

COMPREHENSION: LOOKING FOR MAIN IDEAS

1. b   2. c   3. c

LOOKING FOR DETAILS

1. German immigrants introduced the hamburger to the United States.
2. The 1904 World's Fair was in St. Louis.
3. Most people eat hamburgers on a bun.
4. Most people eat hamburgers at McDonald's.
5. We call convenience foods fast food.
6. The bun and McDonald's made the hamburger a typical American food. McDonald's is a part of nearly every community in the U.S.

UNIT 16

VOCABULARY: MEANING

1. editor   2. public   3. unfortunately
4. praise   5. novel   6. based on   7. various
8. publishing

COMPREHENSION: LOOKING FOR MAIN IDEAS

1. Who is Toni Morrison?
2. Which book won the Pulitzer Prize for Fiction in 1988?
3. When did Toni Morrison win the Nobel Prize for Literature?

LOOKING FOR DETAILS

1. c   2. b   3. c   4. a   5. c   6. b

UNIT 17

VOCABULARY: MEANING

1. gangster   2. heart attack   3. couple
4. Neon   5. license   6. Casinos
7. mispronunciation   8. chapels

COMPREHENSION: LOOKING FOR MAIN IDEAS

1. The hotels in Las Vegas are like another world. The hotels are inexpensive, but they have shows with famous entertainers and restaurants with all-you-can-eat meals.
2. The casinos and hotels have neon lights.
3. Las Vegas has very inexpensive hotels, many wedding chapels, and more churches for its population that any other city in the United States.

LOOKING FOR DETAILS

1. F   2. F   3. F   4. T   5. F   6. T   7. T

UNIT 18

VOCABULARY: MEANING

1. stuck   2. achievements   3. employee
4. reel   5. permanent   6. ceremony
7. billion   8. roles

COMPREHENSION: LOOKING FOR MAIN IDEAS

1. Why do people receive Oscars?
2. What does the reel of film represent?
3. How long has the Oscars ceremony taken place?

LOOKING FOR DETAILS

1. F   2. T   3. F   4. T   5. F   6. T   7. F   8. T

UNIT 19

PREREADING

1. T   2. F   3. F

VOCABULARY: MEANING

1. likely   2. rip up   3. funnel   4. swept
5. twist   6. warn   7. path   8. occur

COMPREHENSION: LOOKING FOR MAIN IDEAS

1. What are tornadoes?
2. Where are tornadoes common?
3. When is the most likely time for a tornado to occur?

LOOKING FOR DETAILS

1. earth → funnel
2. southeasterly → northeasterly
3. cannot → can
4. days → hours
5. 689 → 300
6. Equipment → Nothing
7. hot → dark
8. kill → smash

UNIT 20

PREREADING

1. T   2. T   3. F

VOCABULARY: MEANING

1. deal   2. native   3. doubled   4. purchase
5. expedition   6. route   7. starve   8. guide

COMPREHENSION: LOOKING FOR MAIN IDEAS

1. The Louisiana Purchase was all land between the Mississippi River and the Rockies that President Thomas Jefferson bought from the French in 1803.
2. Lewis and Clark were sent to explore the new land.
3. Sacagawea helped the explorers.

LOOKING FOR DETAILS

1. halved → doubled
2. excluded → included
3. Jenkinson → Jefferson
4. navy → army

5. exhibition → expedition
6. three → two
7. fight → get along with
8. guides → heroes

UNIT 21

VOCABULARY: MEANING

1. slaves   2. continent   3. created
4. seaport   5. homeland   6. contributed
7. festivals   8. on the spot

COMPREHENSION: LOOKING FOR MAIN IDEAS

1. Jazz is a combination of the music of West Africa, the songs the slaves sang, and religions music.
2. Jazz became popular in the United States by the 1920s.
3. People from all over the world play jazz.

LOOKING FOR DETAILS

1. Africa → America *or* to → from
2. bands → homeland
3. festivals → bands
4. Africa → New Orleans
5. spot → part
6. seaport → continent

UNIT 22

VOCABULARY: MEANING

1. grove   2. frost   3. juicy   4. citrus
5. sour   6. lung   7. Climate   8. developed

COMPREHENSION: LOOKING FOR MAIN IDEAS

1. Lue Gim Gong was an immigrant from China who developed sweet oranges.
2. Lue moved to Florida.
3. Lue developed oranges that were very sweet and juicy.

LOOKING FOR DETAILS

1. The Spanish brought orange trees to Florida.
2. Oranges tasted sour in 1500.
3. Lue stayed in San Francisco for three years.
4. Lue became an American citizen in 1877.
5. Fannie Burlingame owned Lue's orange groves before him.
6. Lue received the Wilder Silver Medal from the American Pomological Society.

UNIT 23

VOCABULARY: MEANING

1. sculptor   2. amazed   3. memorial
4. took over   5. carved   6. not over
7. shortly before   8. injured

COMPREHENSION: LOOKING FOR MAIN IDEAS

1. You see George Washington, Thomas Jefferson, Abraham Lincoln, and Theodore Roosevelt.
2. The sculptor was Gutzon Borglum.
3. It took fourteen years to complete the memorial.

LOOKING FOR DETAILS

1. b   2. a   3. b   4. b   5. a   6. b   7. b   8. a

UNIT 24

VOCABULARY: MEANING

1. achieved   2. dormitory   3. giant
4. get over   5. obsession   6. will
7. software   8. dropped out

COMPREHENSION: LOOKING FOR MAIN IDEAS

1. Where did Bill Gates meet his business partner?
2. Why did Bill Gates and Paul Allen create Microsoft?
3. How did Bill Gates achieve his success?

LOOKING FOR DETAILS

1. b   2. b   3. c   4. a   5. b   6. c

UNIT 25

VOCABULARY: MEANING

1. carcasses   2. somewhere   3. build   4. afford
5. farmer   6. mechanic   7. charge   8. race

COMPREHENSION: LOOKING FOR MAIN IDEAS

1. a   2. b   3. a

LOOKING FOR DETAILS

1. T   2. F   3. T   4. F   5. F   6. T   7. T   8. T

UNIT 26

PREREADING

1. T   2. F   3. F

Vocabulary: Meaning

1. berries 2. bush 3. container 4. picking
5. bitter 6. ripen 7. bounce 8. spilled

Comprehension: Looking for Main Ideas

1. A cranberry is a North American fruit that grows on a bush.
2. The cranberry bush grows in northern states like Massachusetts and Wisconsin.
3. John Webb developed the method.

Looking for Details

1. more → less
2. best → bad
3. method → step
4. Americans → settlers
5. Halloween → Thanksgiving
6. cooled → cooked
7. summer → fall
8. easy → hard

UNIT 27

Prereading

1. T 2. T 3. F

Vocabulary: Meaning

1. gray 2. tourist attraction 3. partially
4. architect 5. go through 6. pick
7. originally 8. contest

Comprehension: Looking for Main Ideas

1. The president of the United States lives in the White House.
2. George Washington wanted the White House to be in the nation's capital city.
3. In 1814, the British burned the White House.

Looking for Details

1. b 2. c 3. b 4. c 5. c 6. b

UNIT 28

Vocabulary: Meaning

1. stood for 2. nickname 3. poster 4. fair
5. hired 6. beard 7. look over 8. provide

Comprehension: Looking for Main Ideas

1. a 2. a 3. a 4. a

Looking for Details

1. F 2. T 3. T 4. F 5. T 6. F

UNIT 29

Prereading

1. F 2. T 3. T

Vocabulary: Meaning

1. dust 2. destroyed 3. Bricks 4. droughts
5. Crops 6. plains 7. claim 8. passed a law

Comprehension: Looking for Main Ideas

1. Who were homesteaders?
2. Where did they come to?
3. What did the homesteaders raise?

Looking for Details

1. used → unused
2. nine → five
3. Great Plains → East *or* from → to
4. small → little
5. floods → weather
6. freeze → eat

UNIT 30

Vocabulary: Meaning

1. household name 2. inherited
3. Charities 4. flakes 5. comfortable
6. mail order 7. odd jobs 8. process

Comprehension: Looking for Main Ideas

1. b 2. b 3. a

Looking for Details

1. brother → father
2. Roller → Battle
3. rich → health
4. strange → odd
5. corn → wheat
6. dust → flakes
7. homestead → household
8. family → charities